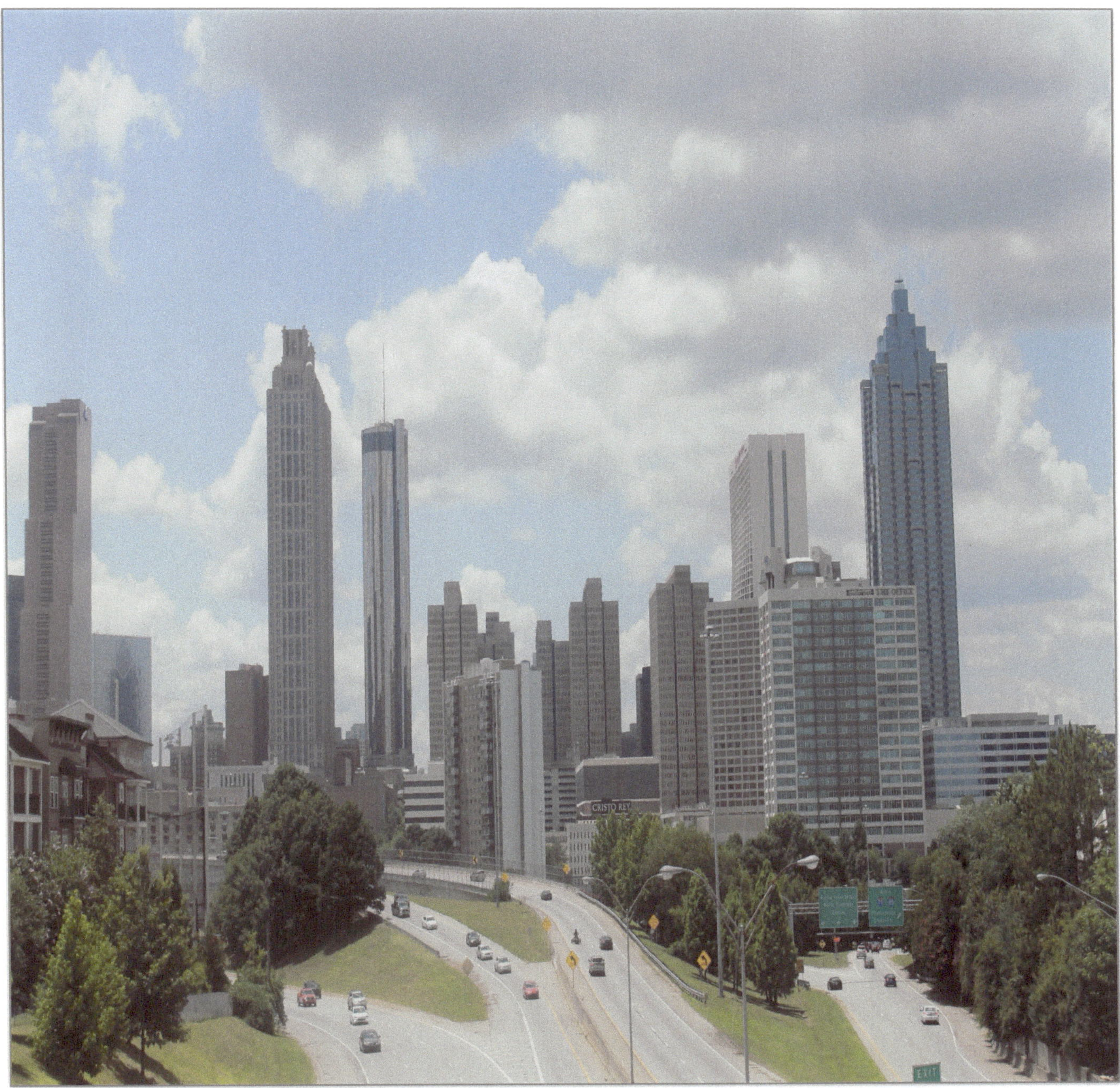
CRISTO REY
THE OFFICE
EXIT

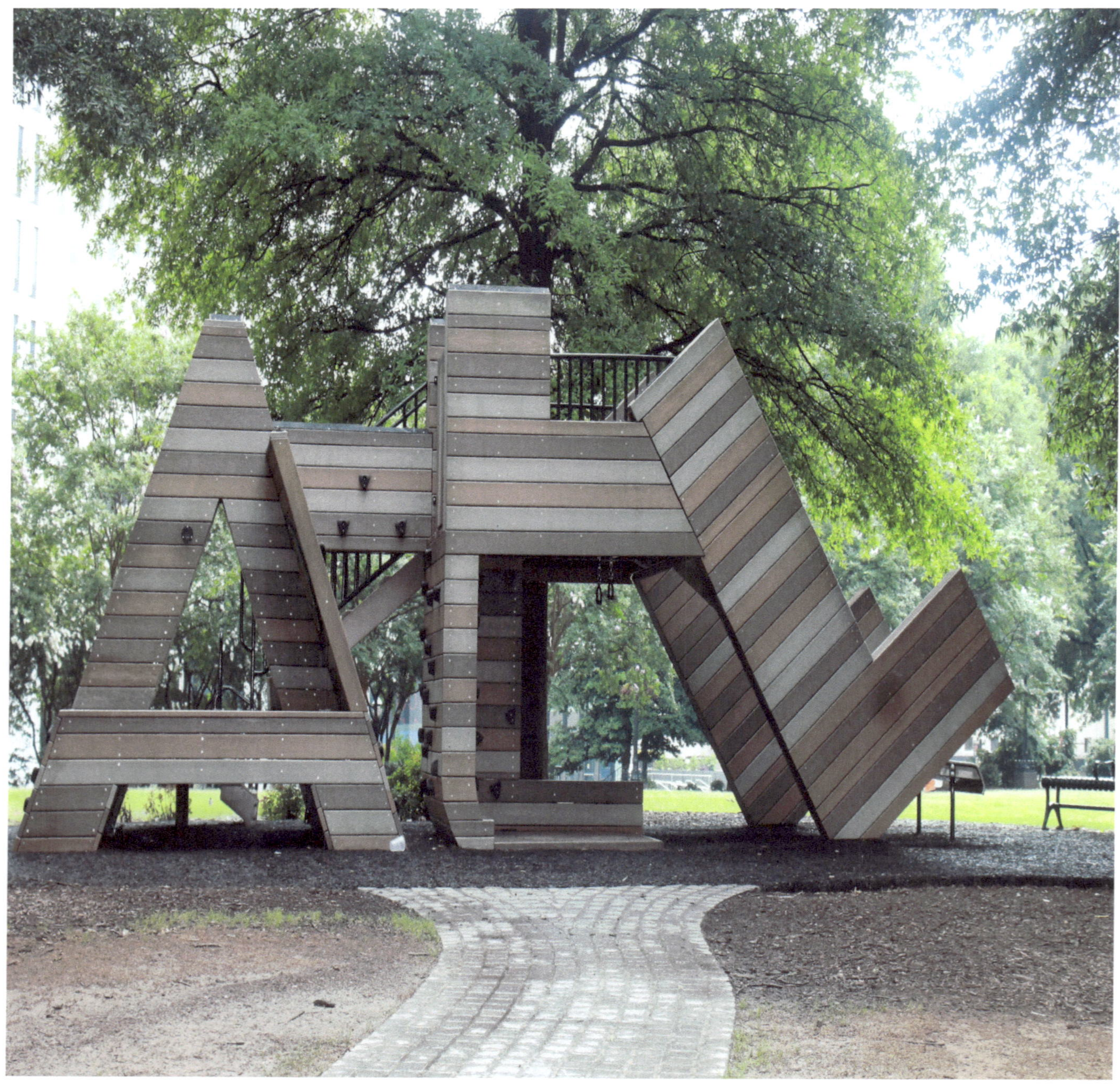

BLACK@LANTA

what you really know about the dirty south?

Francene A. Breakfield

Published in 2020 by Eargasmic Ink. Atlanta Georgia

Cover Designer: Ayanna Card
Cover Photo: Fatima Young (Fatima Michon Photography)

Library of Congress Cataloging-in-Publication Data

ISBN 978-0-578-70847-8

Breakfield, Francene
black@lanta / by Francene Breakfield : introduced by

Pictoral works
Francene Breakfield

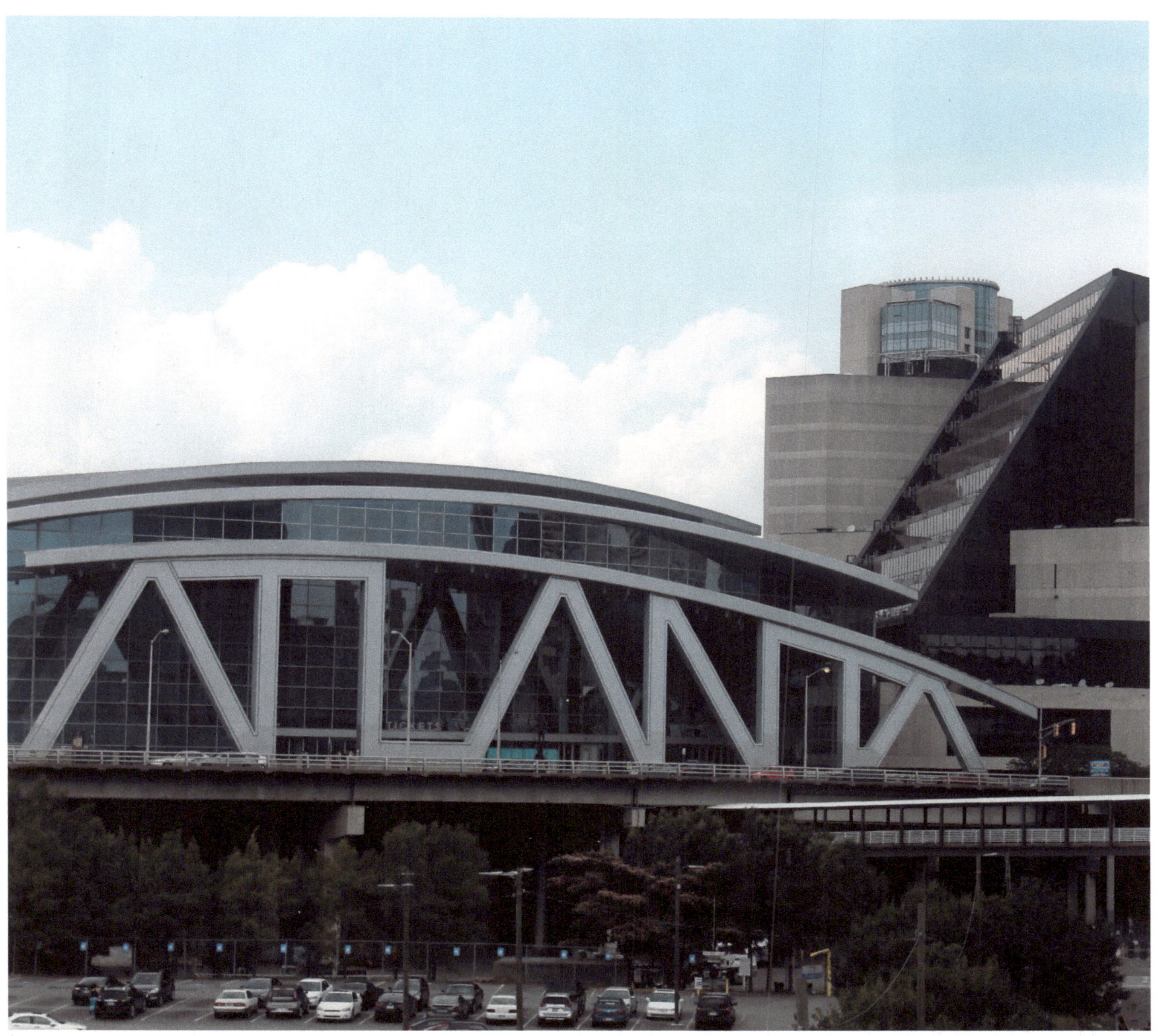
TICKETS

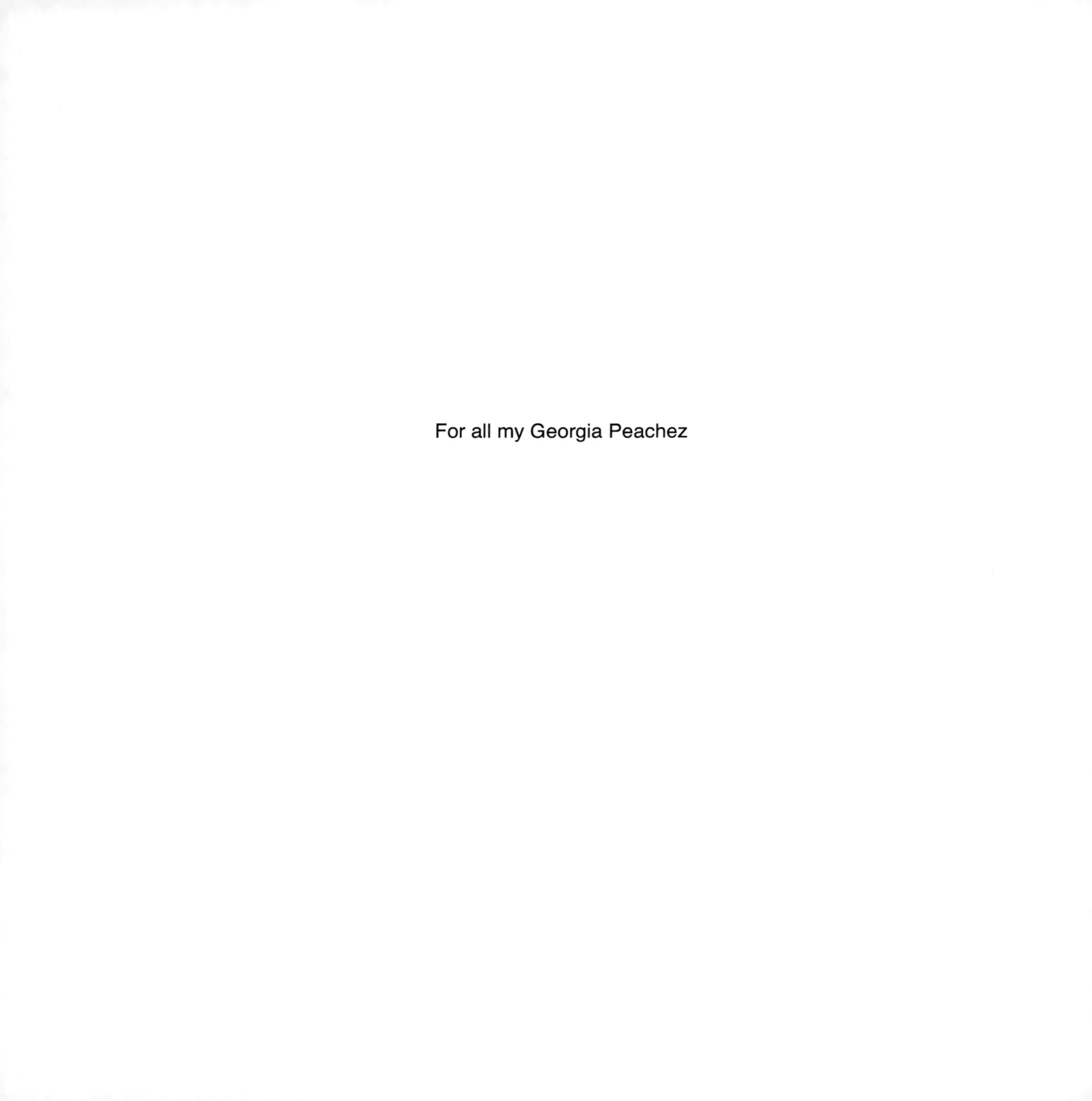

For all my Georgia Peachez

INTRODUCTION

As far back as I can remember, I have been fascinated with maps. When I was about five years old, I saw my very first one while on a family road trip to Detroit, Michigan. Before GPS, drivers had to go to their local gas stations to buy a large 36x36 layout of highways and byways to help them get from point A to point B. On the back of the map was a key to assist the traveler to decipher certain symbols and a small replica of the United States of America. I remember looking for Atlanta on the map. It was not there. I saw Los Angeles, Chicago, Miami, New York City, Houston, and Washington D.C. I was surprised to discover that Atlanta was not considered "major" enough to be included. Why is my city not represented?

Fast forward to September 1990, the beginning of my high school senior year. A pivotal moment in history occurred.There was a press conference held in Tokyo Japan. My mother and I, both sitting on the edge of the couch, were glued to the small color TV set in our living room awaiting an Olympic Committee decision. The commissioner stepped to the podium and announced that the 1996 Olympic Games would be hosted in "The City of ATLANTA." We screamed and hugged each other as if we had won the lottery. We, the city I call home, would be internationally known. These "Olympic Games" would bring money, people, resources, and notoriety. Atlanta was now on the map!

Over the years, Atlanta has been known by many nicknames: The City Too Busy to Hate, The Black Mecca, The City of Trees, HOTlanta, and most recently Black Hollywood. I affectionately call it black@lanta, my city, my home. It is my hope that in this collection of memories, at least one piece resonates in your soul.

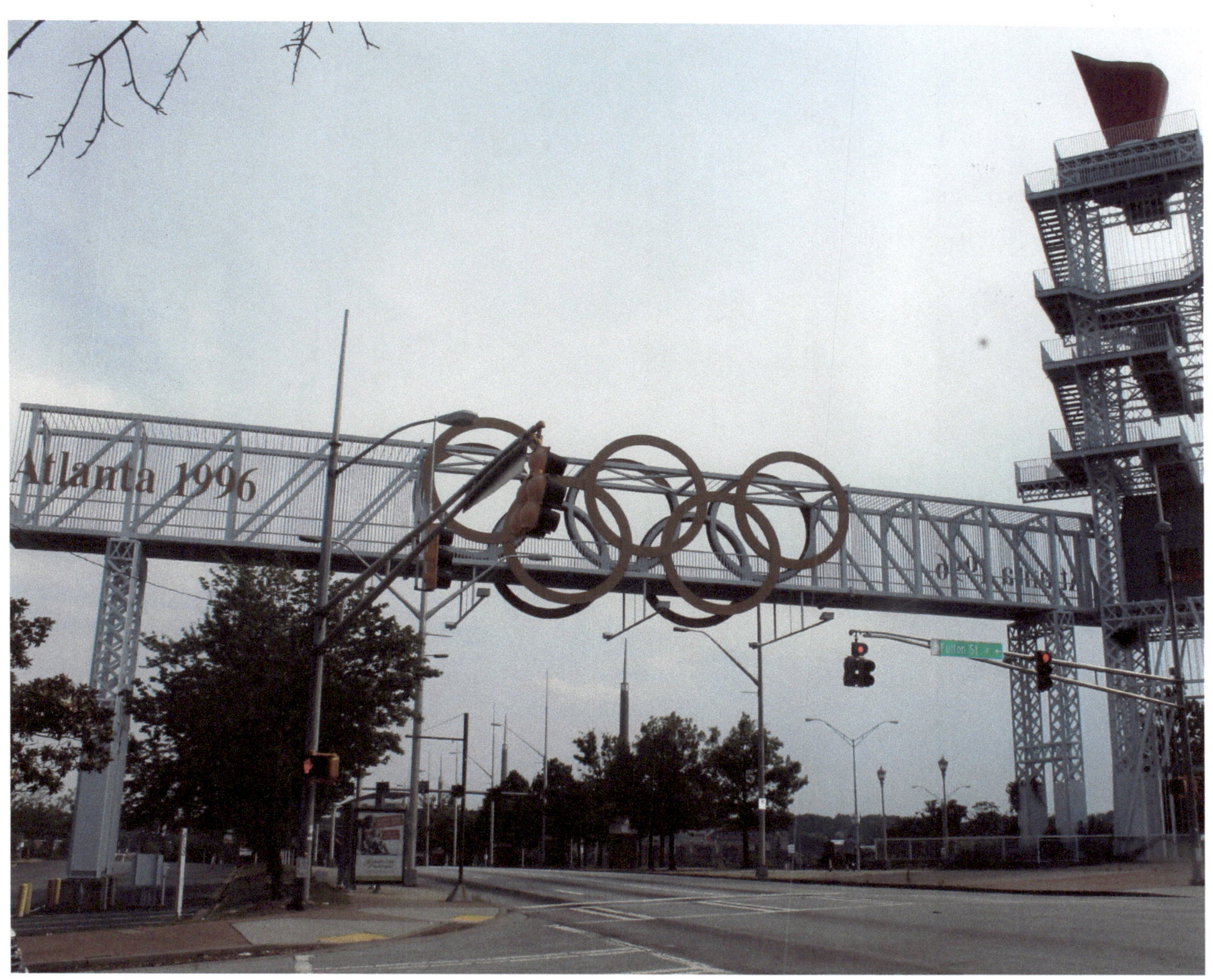
Atlanta 1996
Fulton St

TABLE OF CONTENTS

Dirty South

Goodie Mob asked out of gold toothed mouths
"What y'all niggaz know about the dirty south?"
While some folk affix confederate flags to their ride
As they shout, "Die niggaz!" with their southern pride

The term we use "dirty" may not mean what you think
We aint nasty, we aint ghetto, doesn't mean that we stink
It's the image you have of us. The thought we are less than.
Stereotypical portraits that you paint of a black man

Dirty is the common struggle we've had to live through
Our southern pride comes from our survival and our breakthrough
From slavery to boycotts to police brutality
Fighting for equal rights and our humanity

While Ludacris raps about our southern hospitality
We outchea in these streets trying to hustle and flowality
Just because you thought you knew me, lemme let you know you don't
You can't comprehend the dirty? If you aint from here you won't

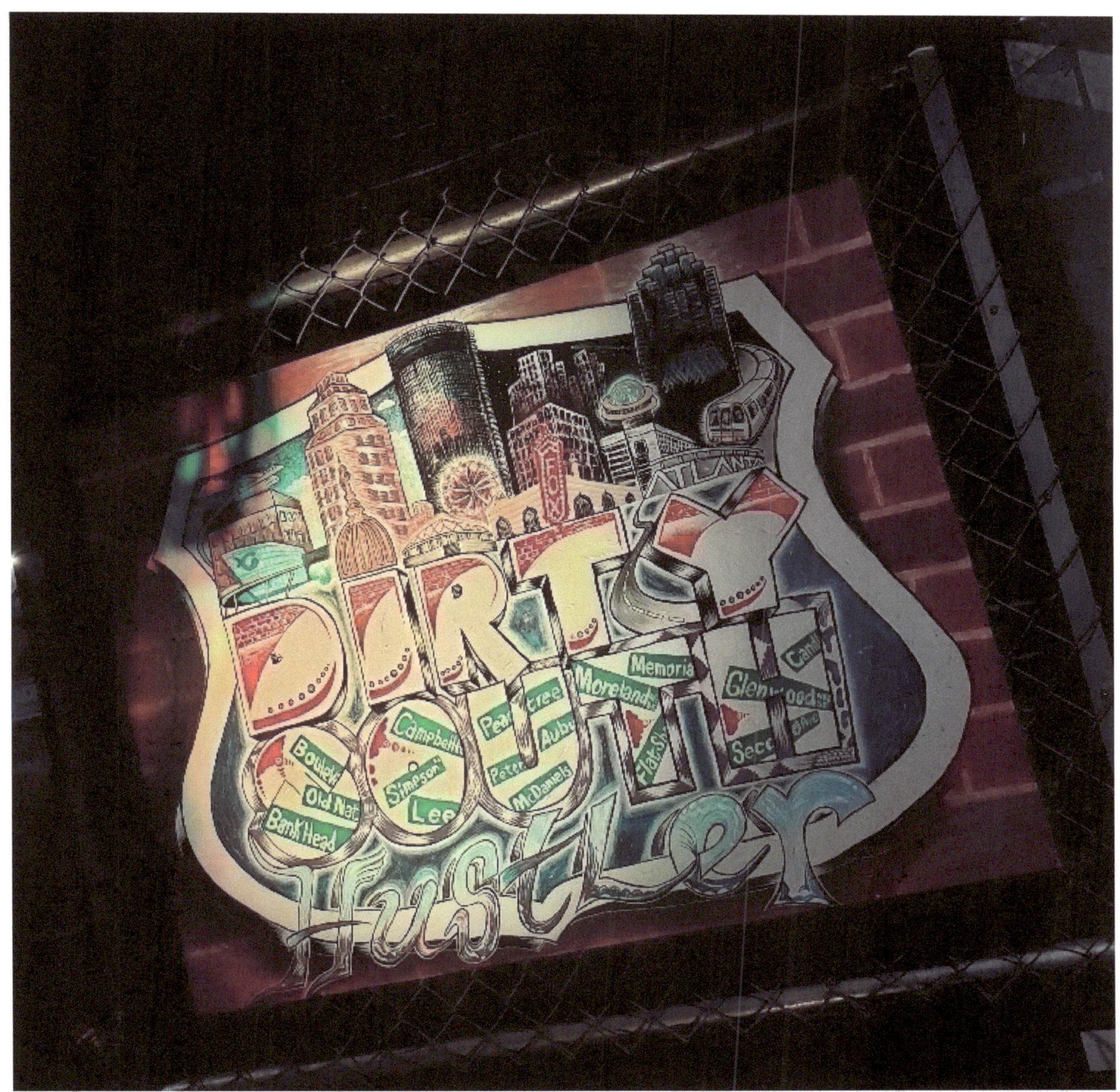

Dirty South
Hustler
Campbellton
Peachtree
Memorial
Moreland
Simpson
Lee
McDaniels
Old Nat
Bank Head

ATLANTA

A city that ascends like a Phoenix from the ashes

Taking flight with open wings soaring upward soaring high

Lights from its skyline look like diamonds in the sky

And even though we come from a segregated past

Never wavering in our fight to be the first and not the last

To be the Black Mecca of America. It is

A place where I call home…The Dirty South

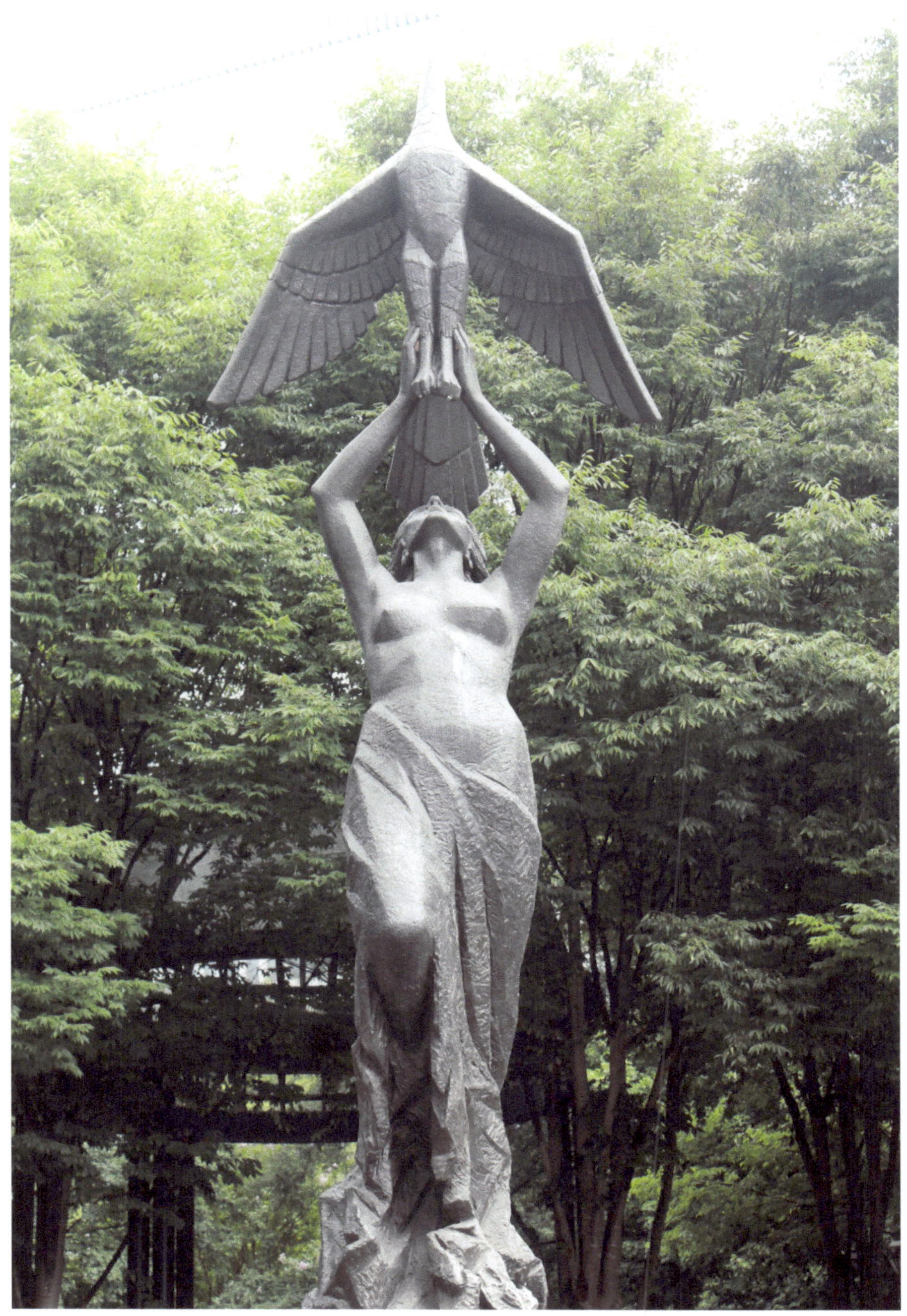

Southern Oaks

Dere's blood on dem dere roots
And dem ol' branches
And de leaves
Of dem dere trees
Dose massive trunks and twisted limbs
Must once had bodies strung in nem
I do believe
as Billie said
"Strange Fruit" strung high
in heat; dey bled
And after all dose years have passed
Dose stains of hate and pain still last
Dose long gray strands of Spanish moss
Rain down like tears
when life is lost
And in my bones
I'll always fear
When dose Great Oaks are standing near

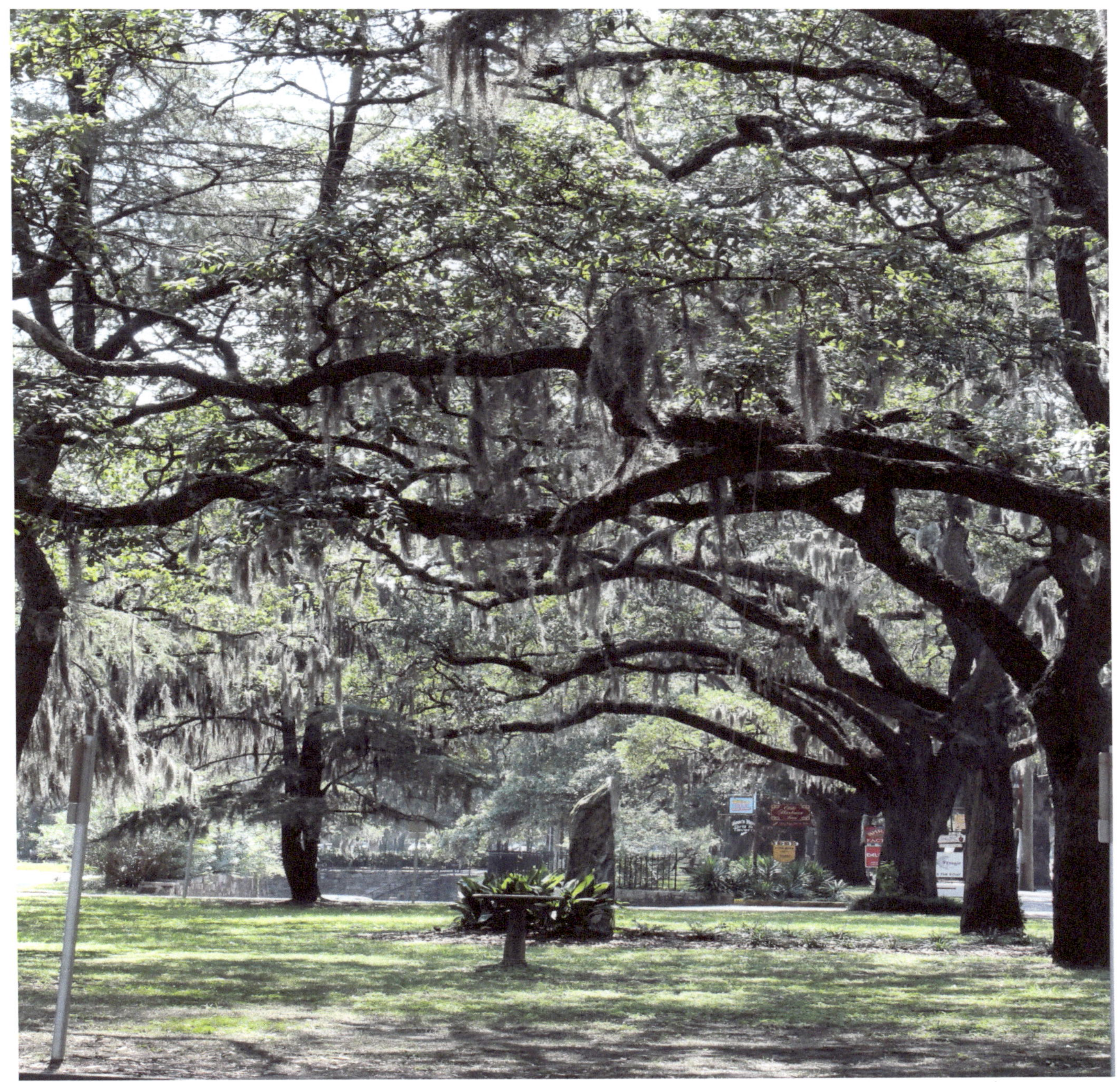

American Pie

Banana, Coconut,

Boston Crème

Fried Apple, Peach

With a scoop of ice cream

Lemon Meringue

Lemon Chess

Lemon Chiffon with

Lemon Zest

Blackbottom, Cheese

Mississippi Mud

Wash it down with milk

Like a Mississippi flood

Key Lime, Pecan, Blackberry

Sweet potato, pumpkin pie

They taste the same to me

Buttermilk, Rhubarb

Cherry a' la mode

Cut me off a slice

Or I can eat it whole

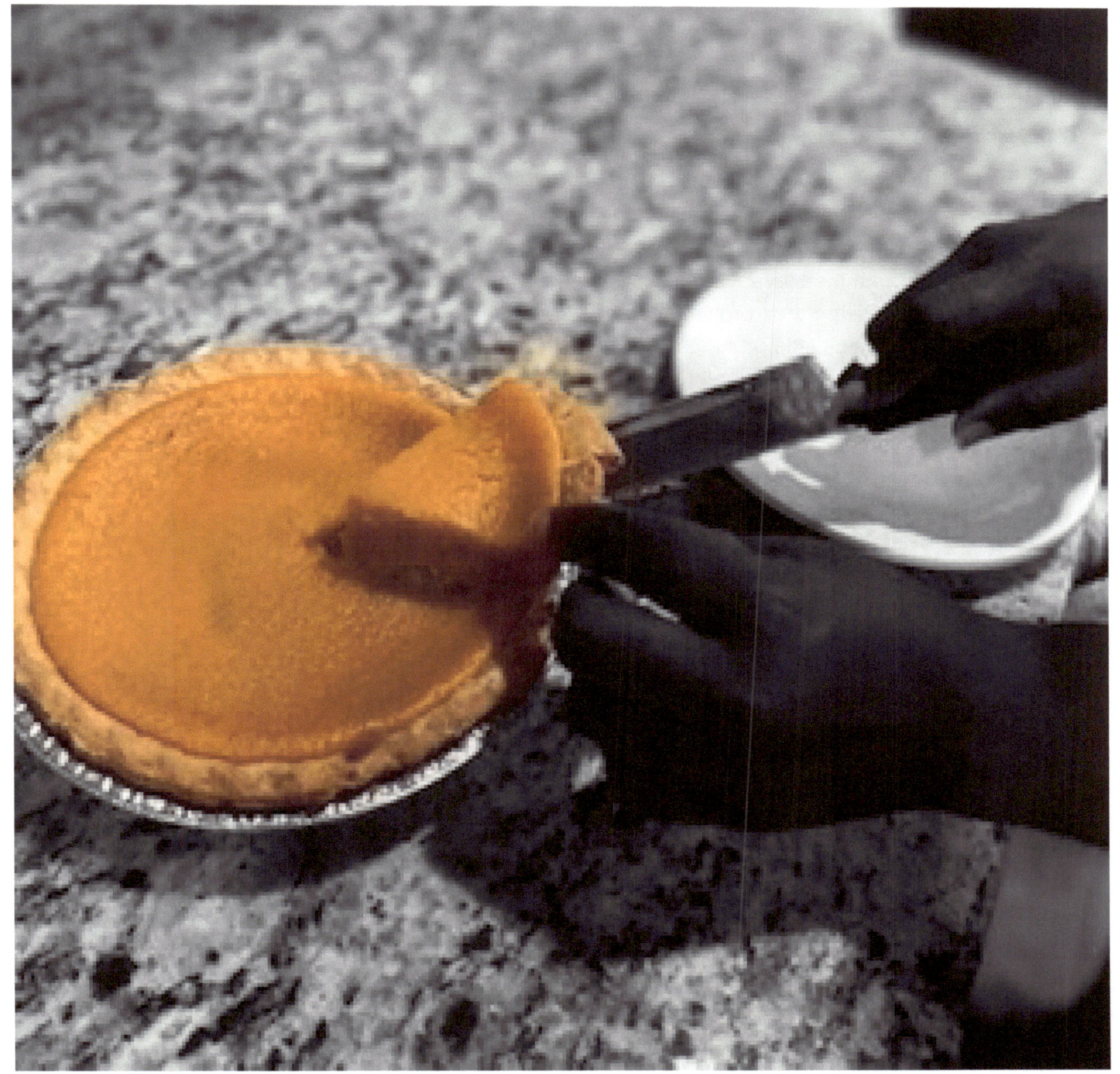

One Drop

its ironic how these racist dixie chicks
have always been in love with them big black dix
for years they hollered rape when they got caught
in the back shed with the slave who they daddy had bought
but now instead of giving their brown faced babies away
they keep their precious little ones cause it's a new day
dem daddies who used to wear pointed White hats
kissing round brown cheeks and pinching baby fat
Unfortunately they think because their skins is White
that their interracial children will receive equal rights
White privilege don't apply when you got brown skin
Some White folks gonna see that afro and know they aint kin
And when they go visit black grandma and run through her grass
She gonna call their whole name fo she spank they black azz

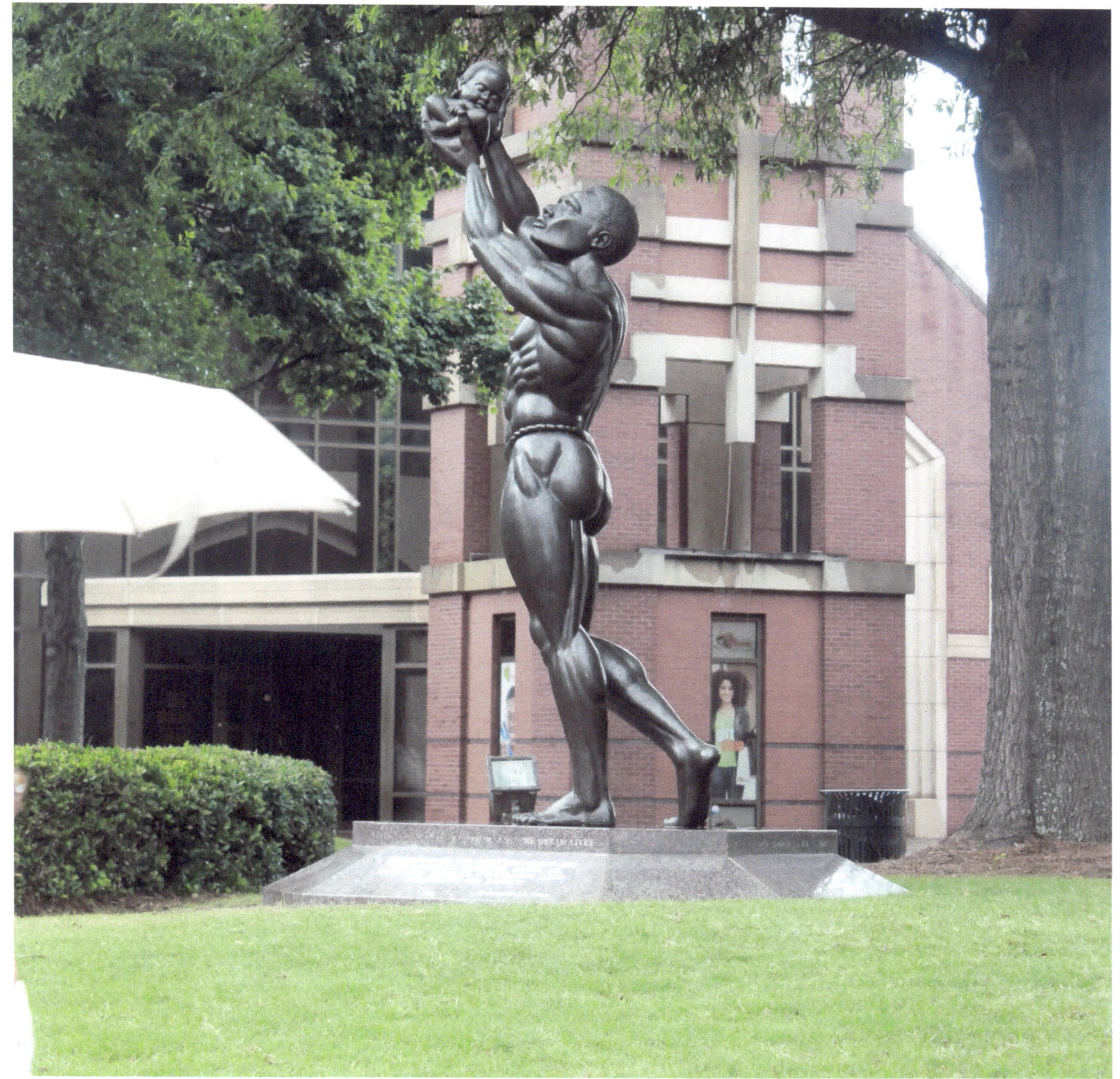

SNS

sundresses sandals big brimmed hats
seersucker suits with bowties and spats
brothers clean from head to toe
walking in the park on the way to the show

nails done, toes did, faces beat
trying not to sweat in this southern heat
permed and press-outs hoping it don't rain
while afro girls rock they curls tryin to maintain

folks come from everywhere far and wide
out of state, down the road to the upper nawf side
of the ATL once a year round mid May
to kick off the summer the dirty south way

You'll see lots of ladies
in their pinks and their green
and some devastating divas
rocking crimson and creme

You will see all shades of purple
with touches of golden hues
Adorned by the brothers
Also known as "The Ques"

Lawn chairs and blankets
is all you need nothing more
Cuz they got plenty of drink tickets
And food trucks galore

Quinn and the Jukebox
are guaranteed to entertain you
While the Stews keep it 2 Live
As they rep the Delta Mu Mu

All the monies raised go towards
a noble cause and deed
Gifting scholarships to students
who have financial need

The venue will be packed
so don't you dare be late or tardy
It's the owtest soiree of the year
Let's get down and party hardy

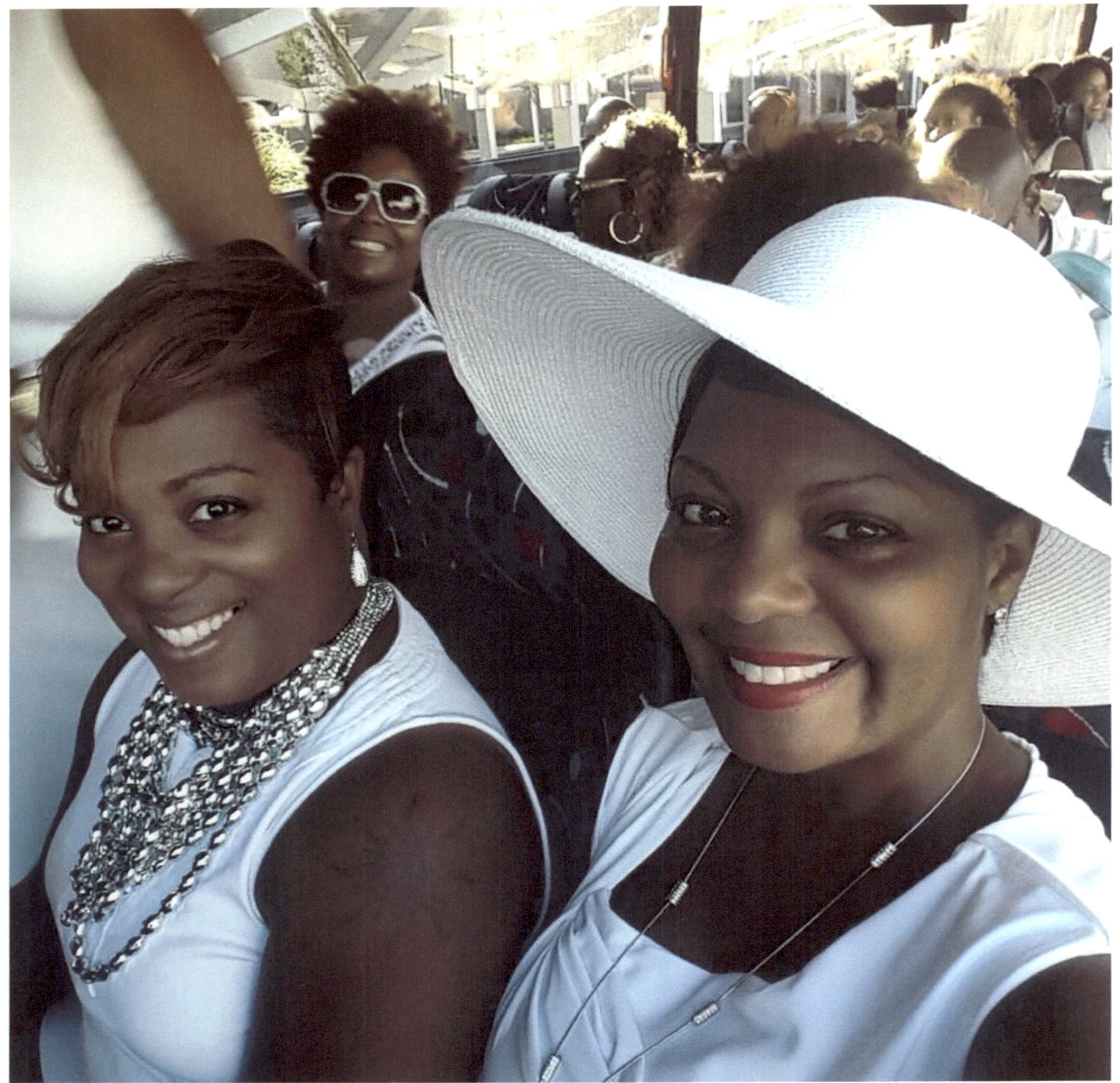

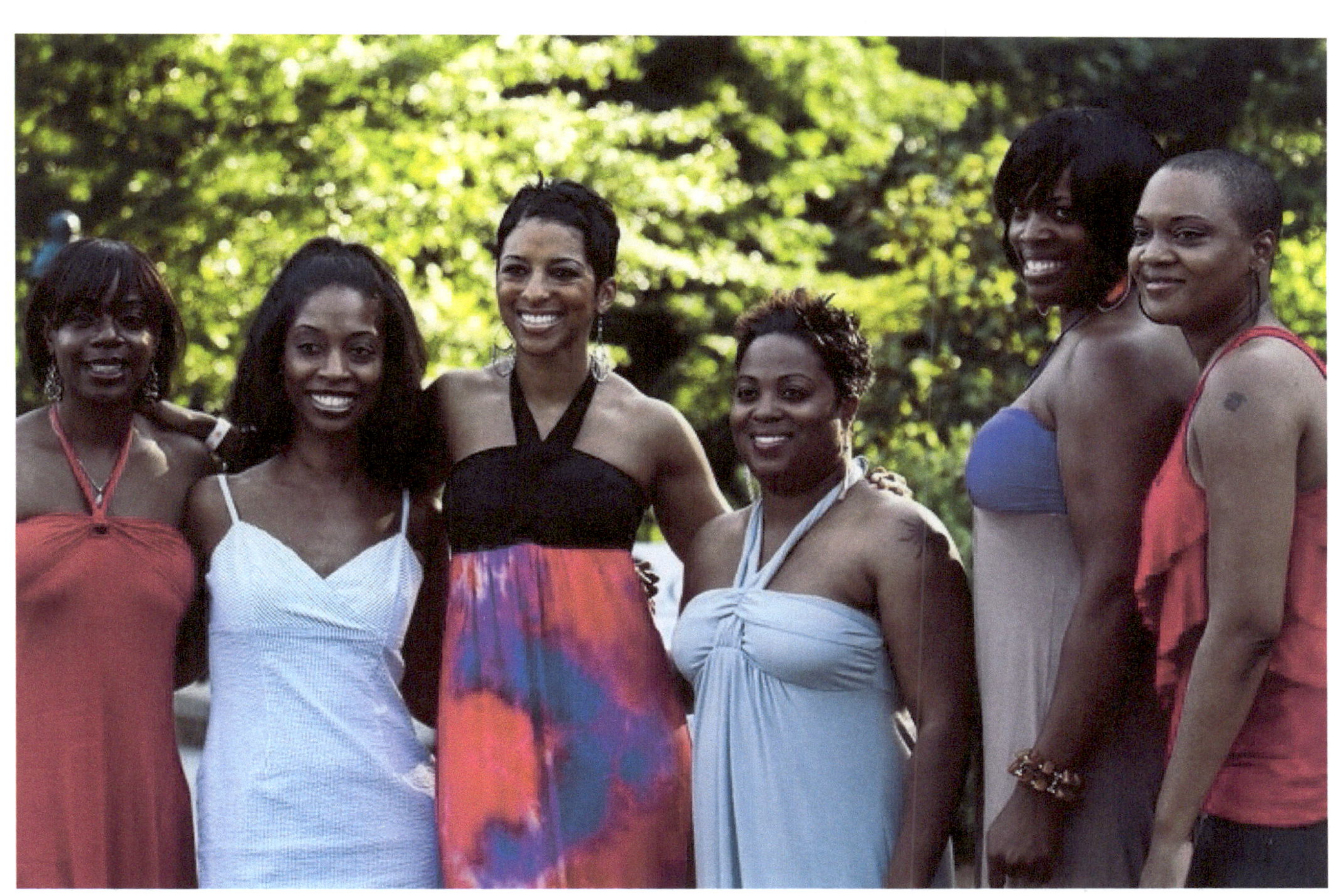

Suga

diabetes is what they call it
scientist can't seem to solve it
pills and needles all I see
and visits to the pharmacy

co-pays several times a year
a cure for all ain't no time near
they want us to take all these meds
or is that doubt just in my head

i don't feel good i don't feel well
i'm overwhelmed i want to yell
exercise and diet they say
will help your suga go away

but seems like everywhere I turn
there's calories that I gotta burn
cause all the food is sugar filled
eating out gon' get me killed

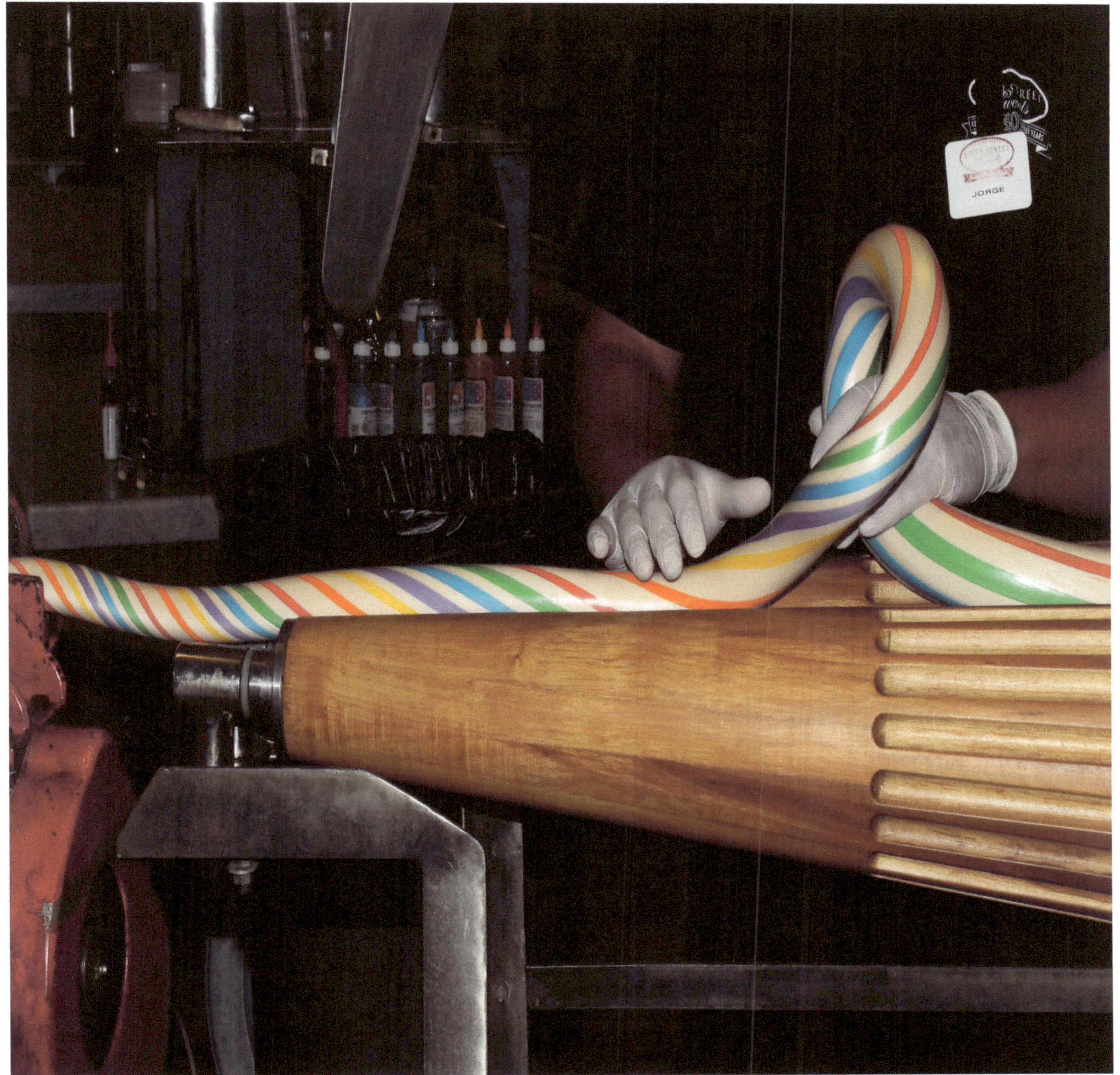
JORGE

We are ATLien, Georgia peach, wearin' nem
Adidas we bought from walters, on our feet
as we step over homeless folk, thats sound asleep
on piedmont, northside, and peachtree street

we got dem hawks, dem braves, dem dirty bird falcons
had dominique, vick, and the legend hank aaron
They tried to bring trophies home but the cards were stacked against em
And fans are fair-weather like a johnny gill anthem

martin luther king is more than just a street here
this is his birthplace, his body lies in heat here
Georgia red clay turn our white keds orange
while the potholes in these streets keep our car tires worn

When you on the north west side, it’s unbeweavable
The number of liquor stores is inconceivable
Baptist churches sit, on every corner
Yet sinners still sinning and preachers still warning ya

Buckhead, Bankhead cross the tracks
One housed rich white folk, the latter poor Blacks
Old skool money mansions and private schools
versus housing projects, full of folks with da blues

If you aint have insurance you sho was born at Grady
All the other hospitals were too bougie or just too shady
To take our kind of people with they chocolate faced babies
Or you could just stay at home and call the midwife lady

We claim Outkast, Lil Jon,T.I.,TLC
Luda, Usher, Goodie Mob, and Jermaine Dupree
Through their music you can learn, about the dirty south
As rap lyrics and ballads, come out they dirty mouths

Spelman, Morehouse, Clark AU, Mo Brown
were choices of colleges you could attend in town
After integration, you could go to Georgia State
Or even Georgia Tech, if you had a real high GPA

Greenbriar, West End, and South Dekalb Mall
is where our parents shopped to get our clothing and all
And if you had a little money, you could go to Lenox Square
Or shop at Rich's Downtown to get your Sunday ware

We are ATLien from the SWATs tellin nem
transplants that move here thats always complain
Take yo azz back from whereseneva you came in
Don't be bad moufin my city, cuz we're freakin amazin

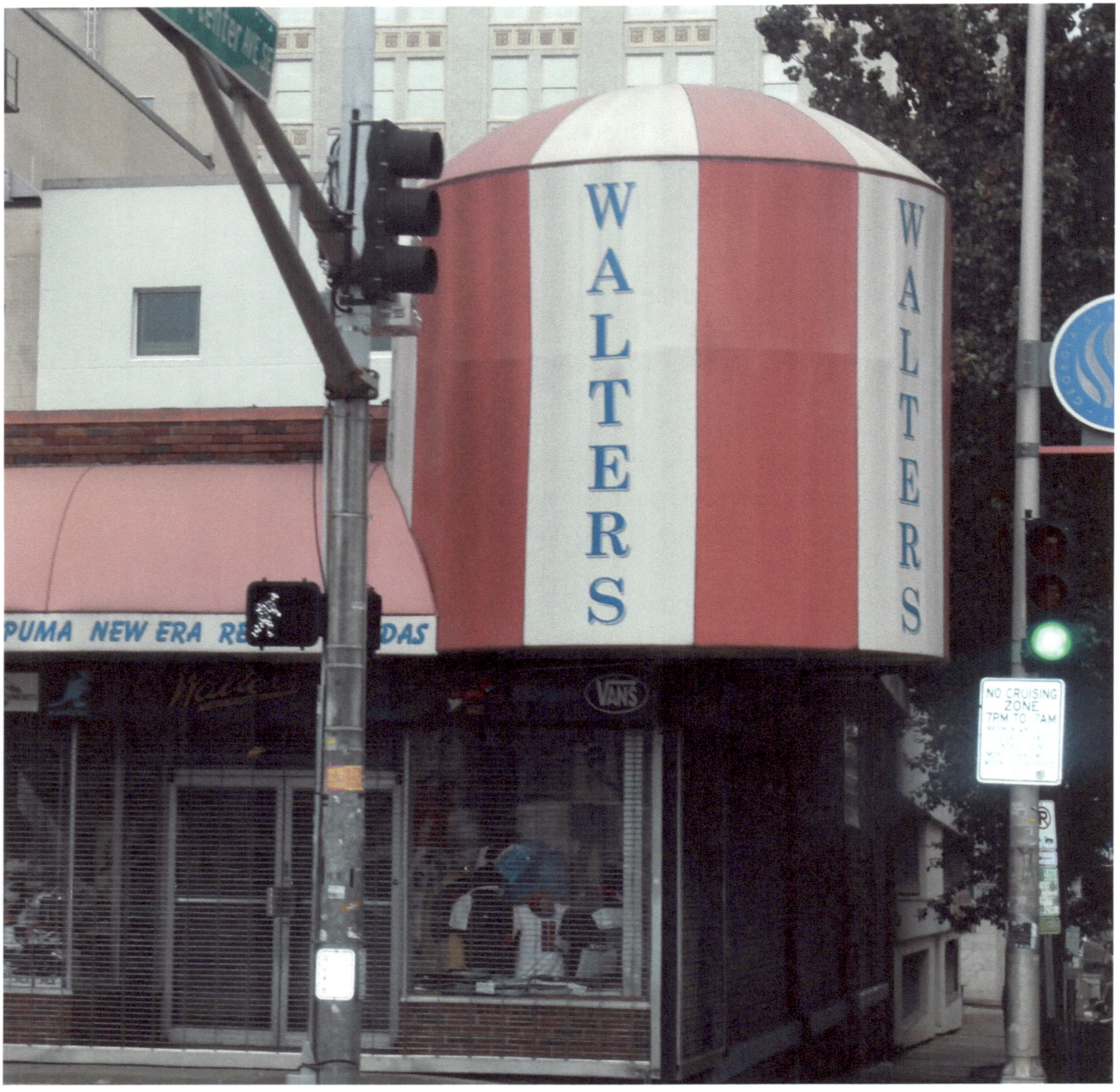
WALTERS
WALTERS
PUMA NEW ERA
VANS
NO CRUISING ZONE 7PM TO 7AM

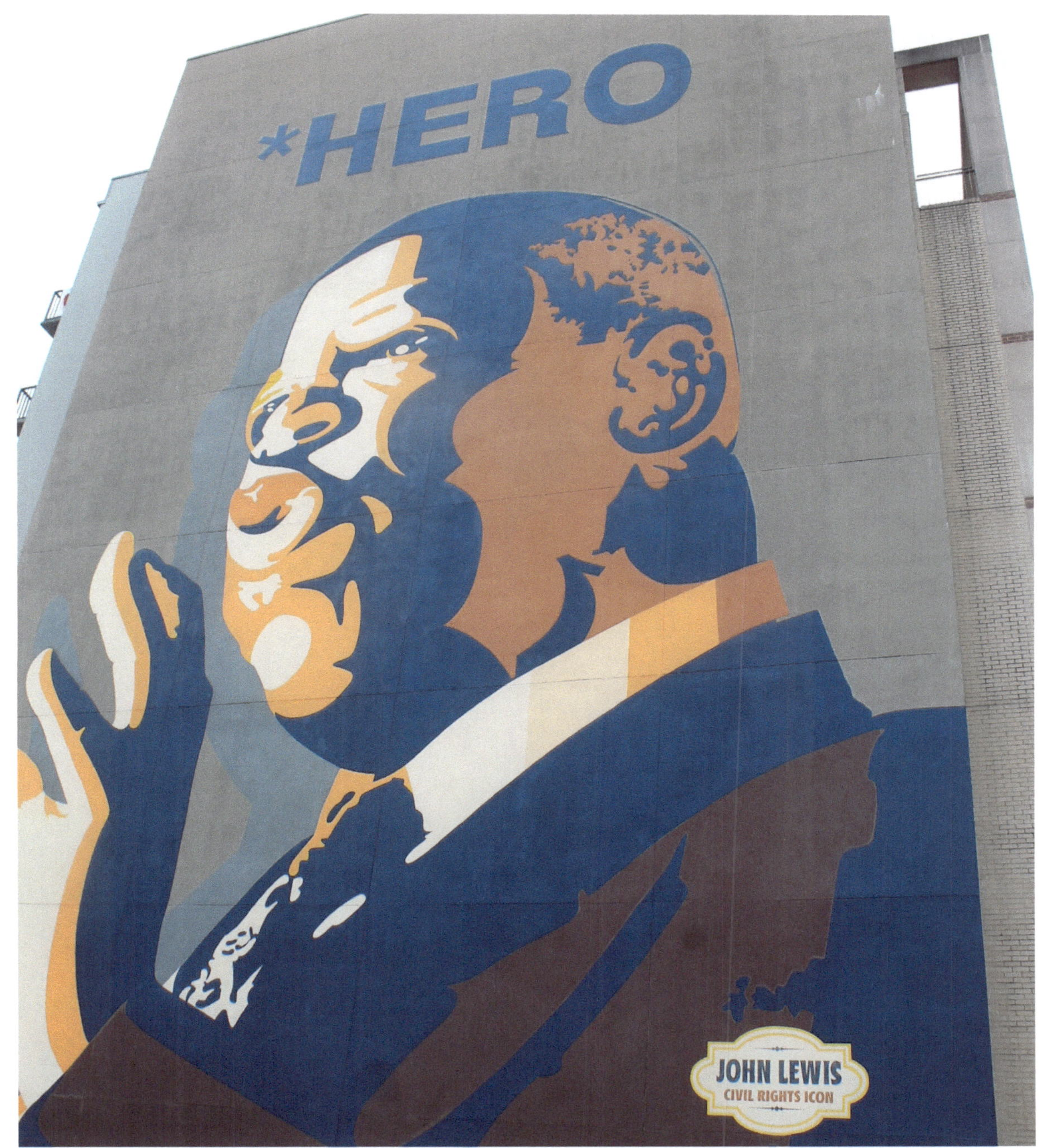
*HERO
JOHN LEWIS
CIVIL RIGHTS ICON

School House Rocks

Mays High, Doug,
Harper, and Northside,
Brown, Crim, Fulton,
George High, and Southside.

Carver, Grady,
Turner, North Fulton,
Archer, Sylvan, Therrell,
Washington, and West Fulton

That is where
we were edumacated
Before cheating scandals and
charter schools were created

We had teachers who cared
bout the goals that we stated
and made sure we learned something ‘
before we graduated

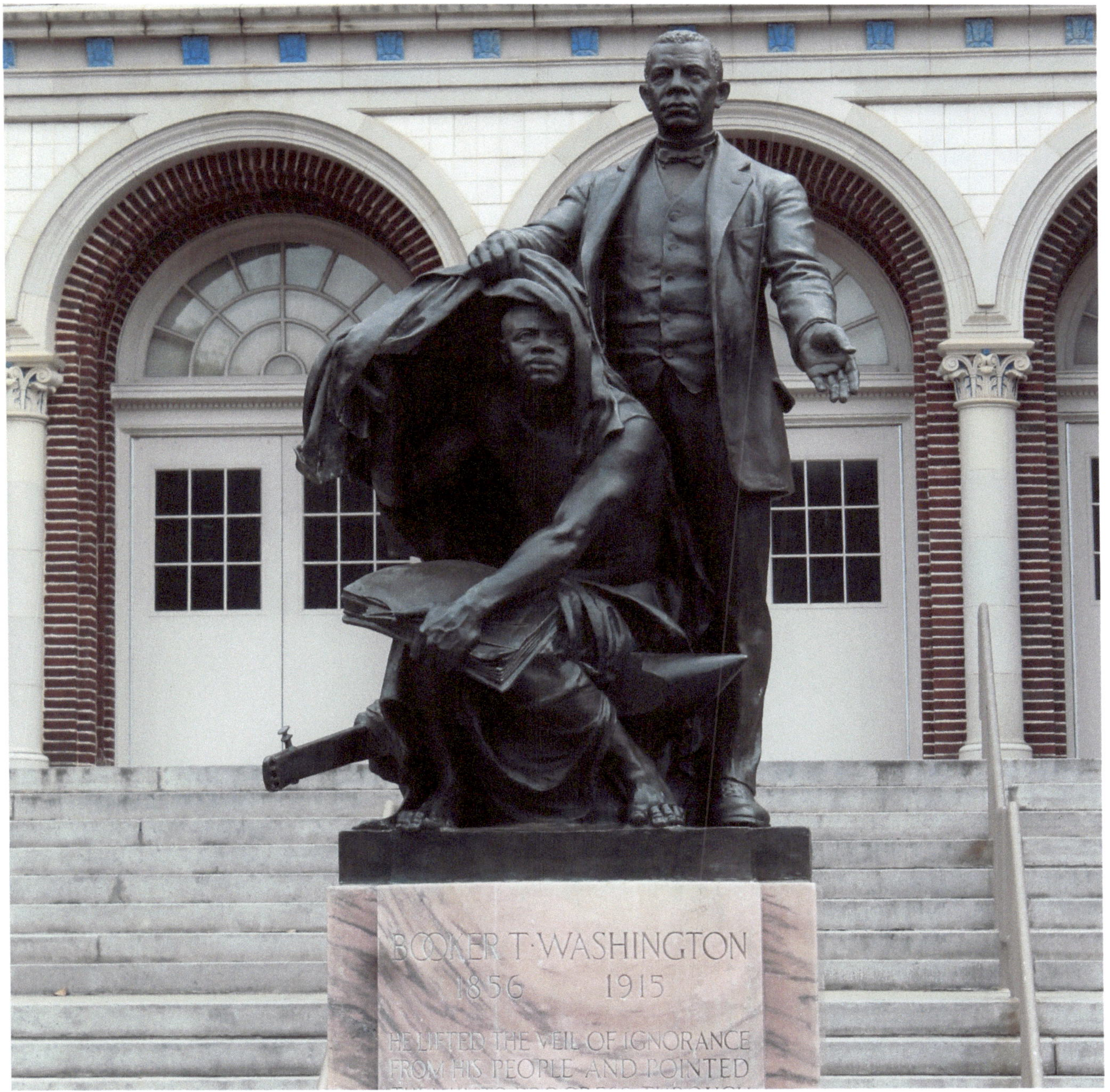
BOOKER T. WASHINGTON
1856 1915
HE LIFTED THE VEIL OF IGNORANCE
FROM HIS PEOPLE AND POINTED

Aint Nothing REAL about REALity TV

So what chu think about these REAL Housewives?

These women acting REAL yet living fake lives

This mess being broadcast, televised to the masses

To fog up the lenses of everyone's glasses

The reality of it all is we was REAL House Nigguhz

Now we're teaching our young girls how to be gold diggers?

We still in the Big House, we still in the field

Enslaving our own minds claiming we "keeping it REAL"

So Harriett and Rosa and Coretta and the like

Fought for women to vote and to have equal rights

For what? To have the right and not go to the polls

For the opportunity to be CEO's but we rather be hos?

How much are actors getting paid to sell all our souls?

What were writers thinking when they created these roles?

Let's play into the stereotype that Black women fight

They're angry and they're bitter, they hate themselves right?

They all wear weave and live way beyond their means

I mean that's what's portrayed on MY television screen

Shouldn’t we be angry at Mona Scott Young
For producing these shows that make us look dumb?
Or angry at ourselves for watching this shiid
VH-1 and Bravo say, “Viewers made it a hit!”

Because “Sorority Sisters” don’t represent my sisterhood
Ain’t no LOVE in “Love and Hip Hop” and Atlanta ain't da hood
The birthplace of a King and The Home of the Braves
Is now the Home of the Ratchet and The New Age Slave?
So I challenge you to think, don’t play into their games
The media’s not your teacher, it’s supposed to entertain
Turn away from negativity, don’t even take a second look
Turn the channel, or better yet...turn it off, and read a book

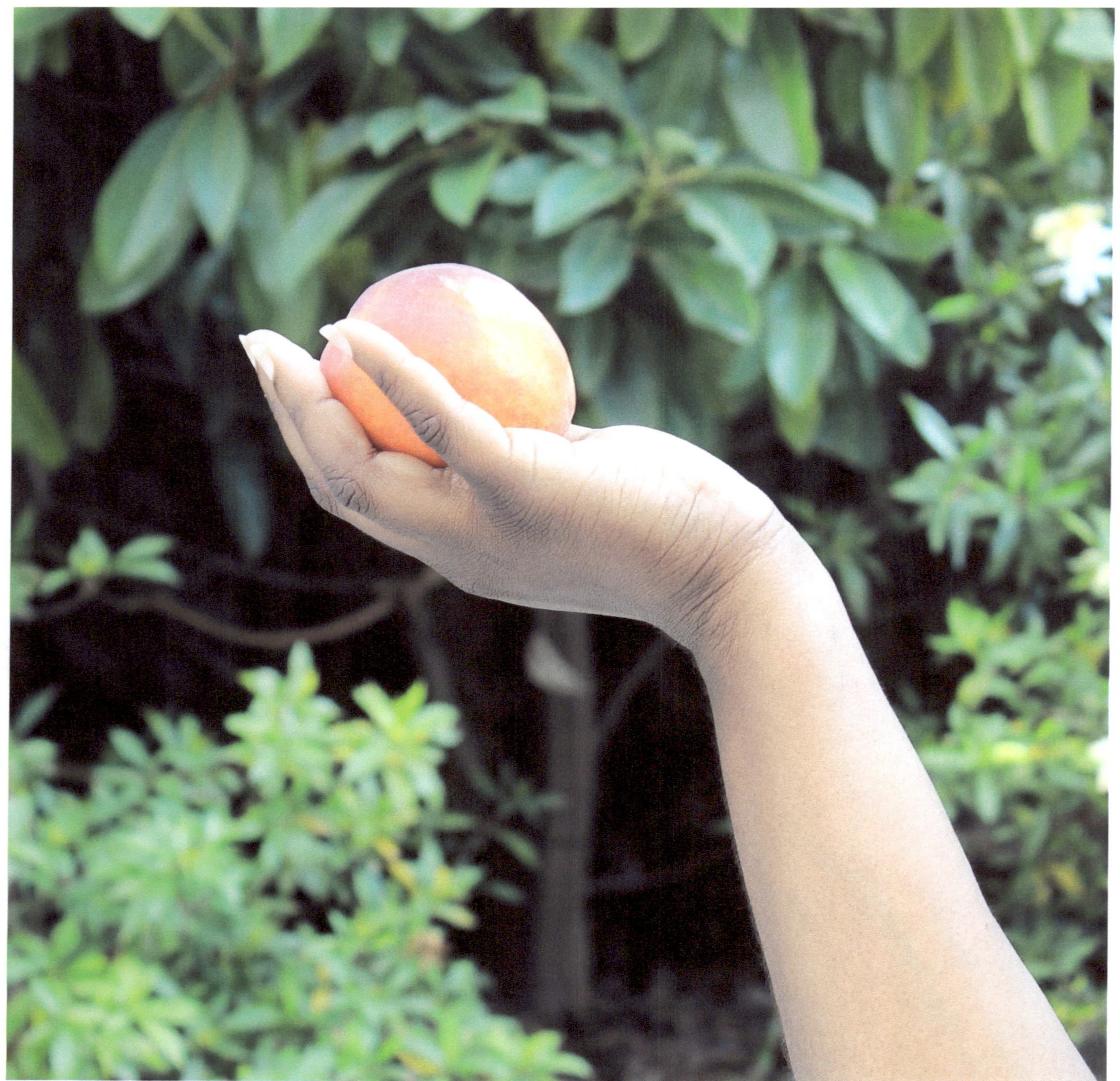

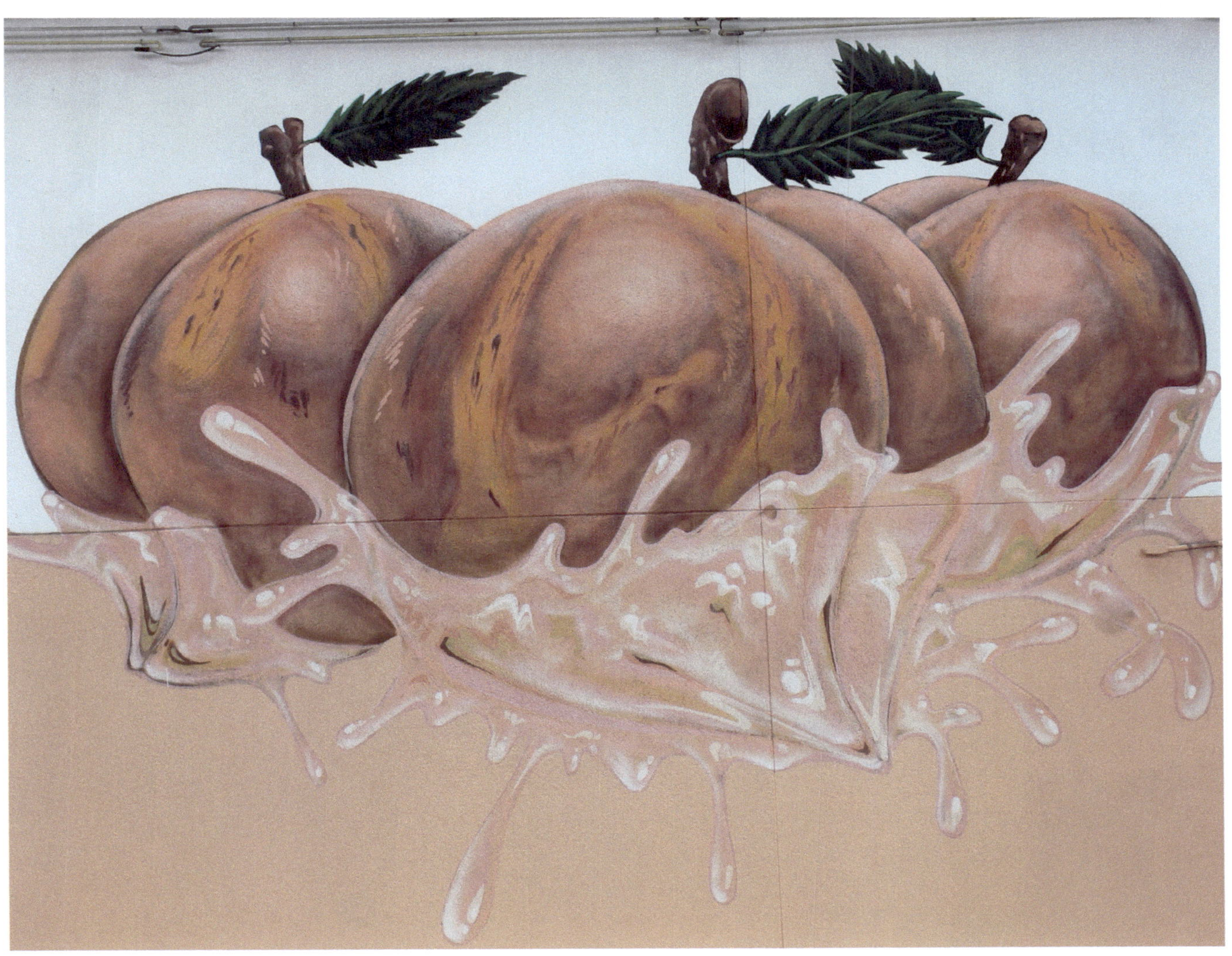

The Flagship

in 1785
the first state college was incorporated

in 1804
its first class graduated

in 1918
women matriculated

and in 1961
they were desegregated

something changed in that year
a higher ed institution with an all white atmosphere

went from red to black in the blink of an eye
Hamilton and Hunter uprooted their lives

to make a difference; they made history
they fought the good fight, so that kids like me

from the ATL and far and wide
could go to any school that their heart desired

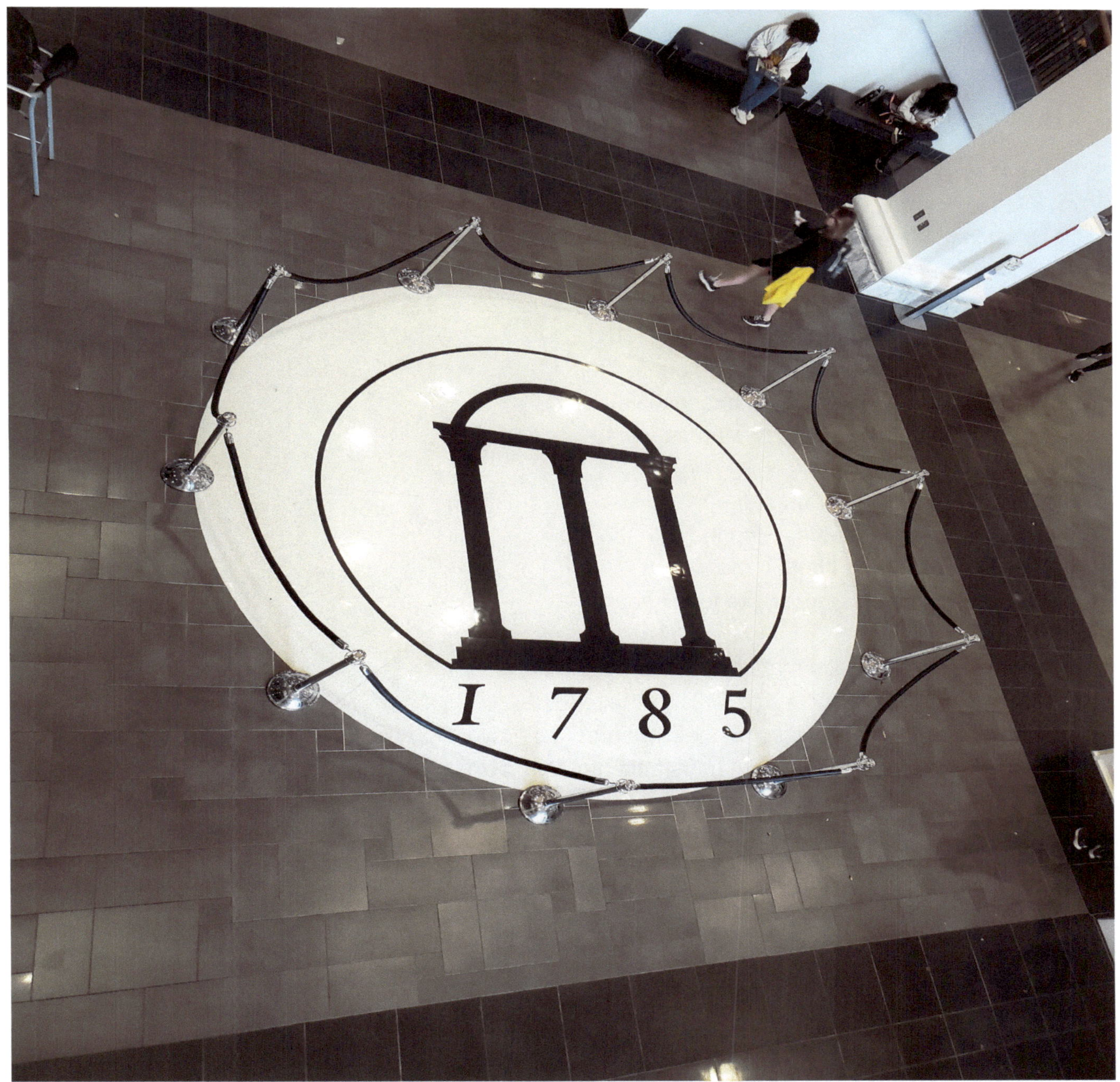
1785

Integrated but segregated

I went to an all Black school with all Black teachers
An all Black church with a pro-Black preacher
We lived in the hood where I had all Black friends
Went shopping at the Black Mall known as the West End

People ask me, “Why didn’t you go to a HBCU?”
My daddy went to Mo’Brown; Mom went to Clark U
Dad said, “Go to a white school because you can
I didn’t have that option in the South as a man

Of color and nor did your mother”
He said,“Be uncomfortable. Integrate with the other”
So what did I do when I got on the yard?
I found a Black church that spoke to my heart

I found a Black hair stylist that could style my Black hair
I pledged a Black sorority and found sisterhood there
Found the only Black professor in the Department of Psychology
Became her intern so that I could have a mentor that looked like me

So even though I may have been the only brown face
in most of my classes and I felt out of place
I still segregated myself so I would have peace of mind
Like the kids in the cafeteria who sit wit they kind

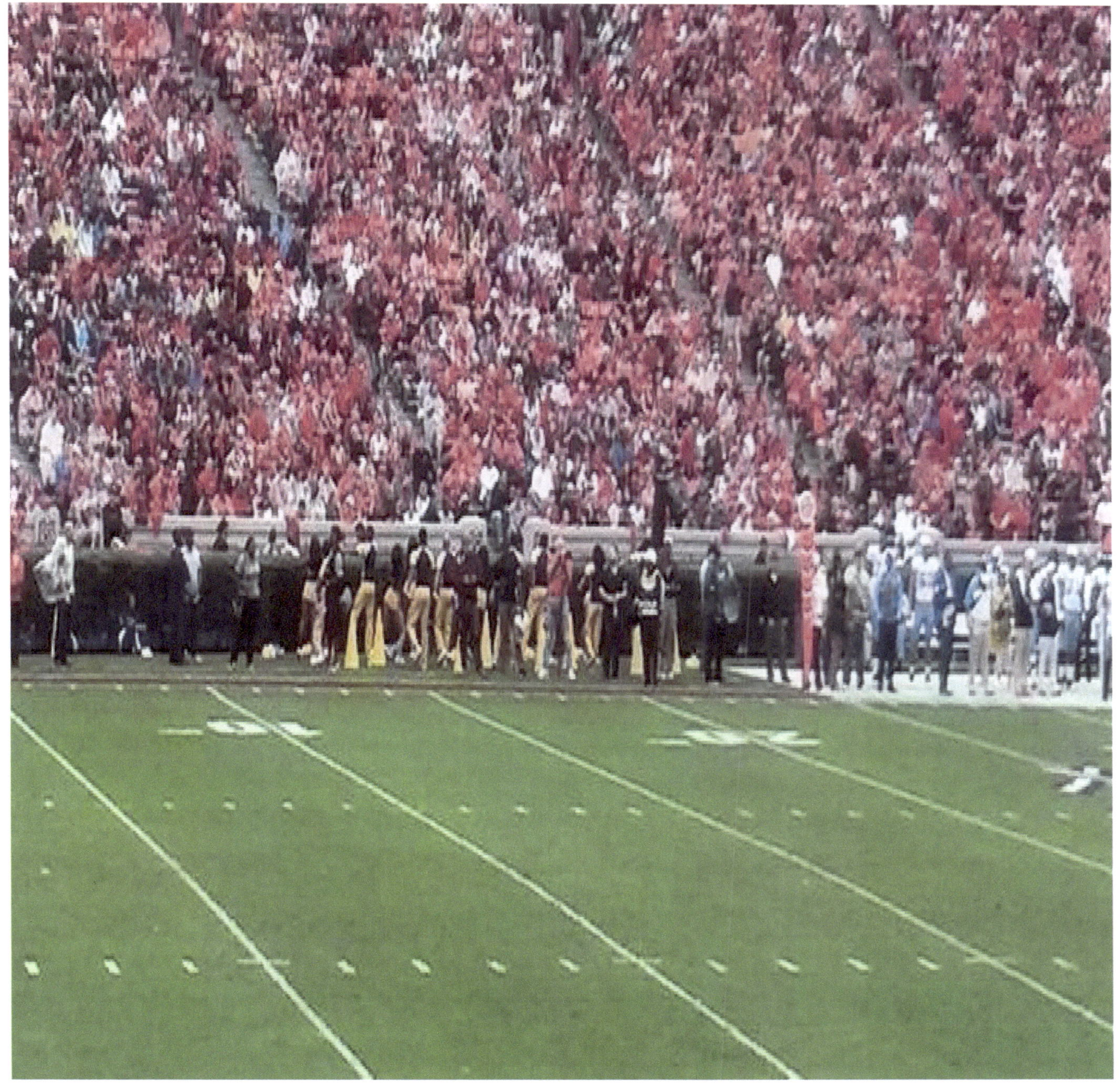

Proud to Be

When I say I got Atlanta Pride
People look at me sideways
and say that I must be swimming
in rainbows
and walk in parades
down peachtree street
oh you must be gay
or that's what they say
When I say I got Southern Pride
They say "You can't have that!"
You don't own a confederate flag
You aint po white trash
You don't reside in a trailer park
And wear all white after dark
You don't know our way
or that's what they say
When I say I got Black Pride
They ask if I was a part
of the Black Lives Matter Movement
They shout Wakanda Forever and say
You a radical girl
You don't like whites
That's why you rocking that afro
You cray cray
or that's what they say
So what do I say to let everyone know
That I love my city?..It's ATLHOE
Imma represent the Peace up A Town Down
Til I close my eyes and get laid in the ground

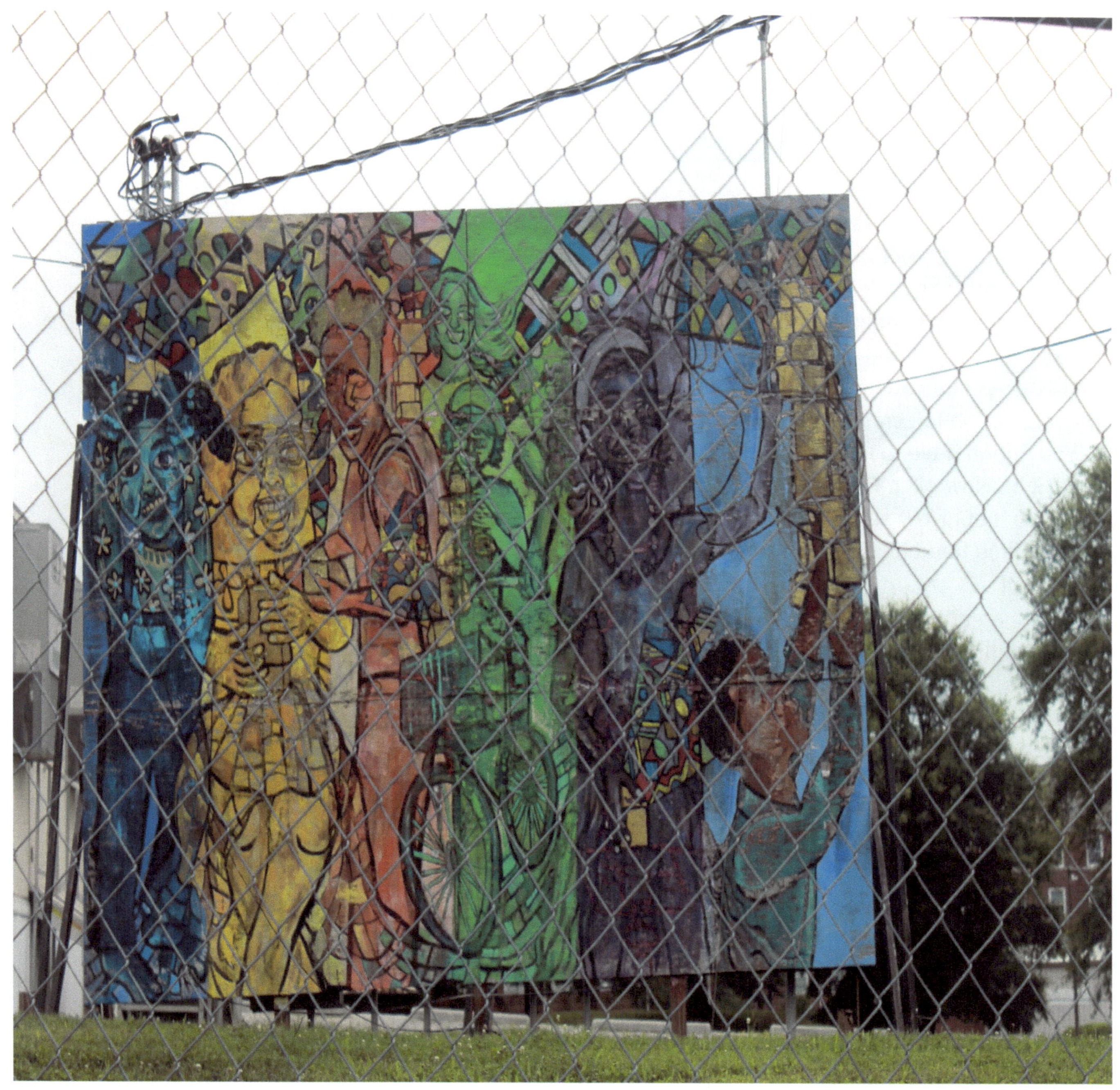

YEEK!

1 and 2 and you know what to do CLAP!
Right, left, right Yeek!
Left, right, left Yeek!
Move your feet Yeek!
Now freeze 2 3 Yeek!
Skate ah ah
Hit them knees ah hah
Crank to the left crank to the right
You gonna have to keep it tight
Git it in. Now git it. Rag top!
Shake it up. Now shake it. Wussup?
Face face head head shoulder shoulder
gut butt
Ah ah, ah ah
Ahhhhhhhhhhh

YEEK!

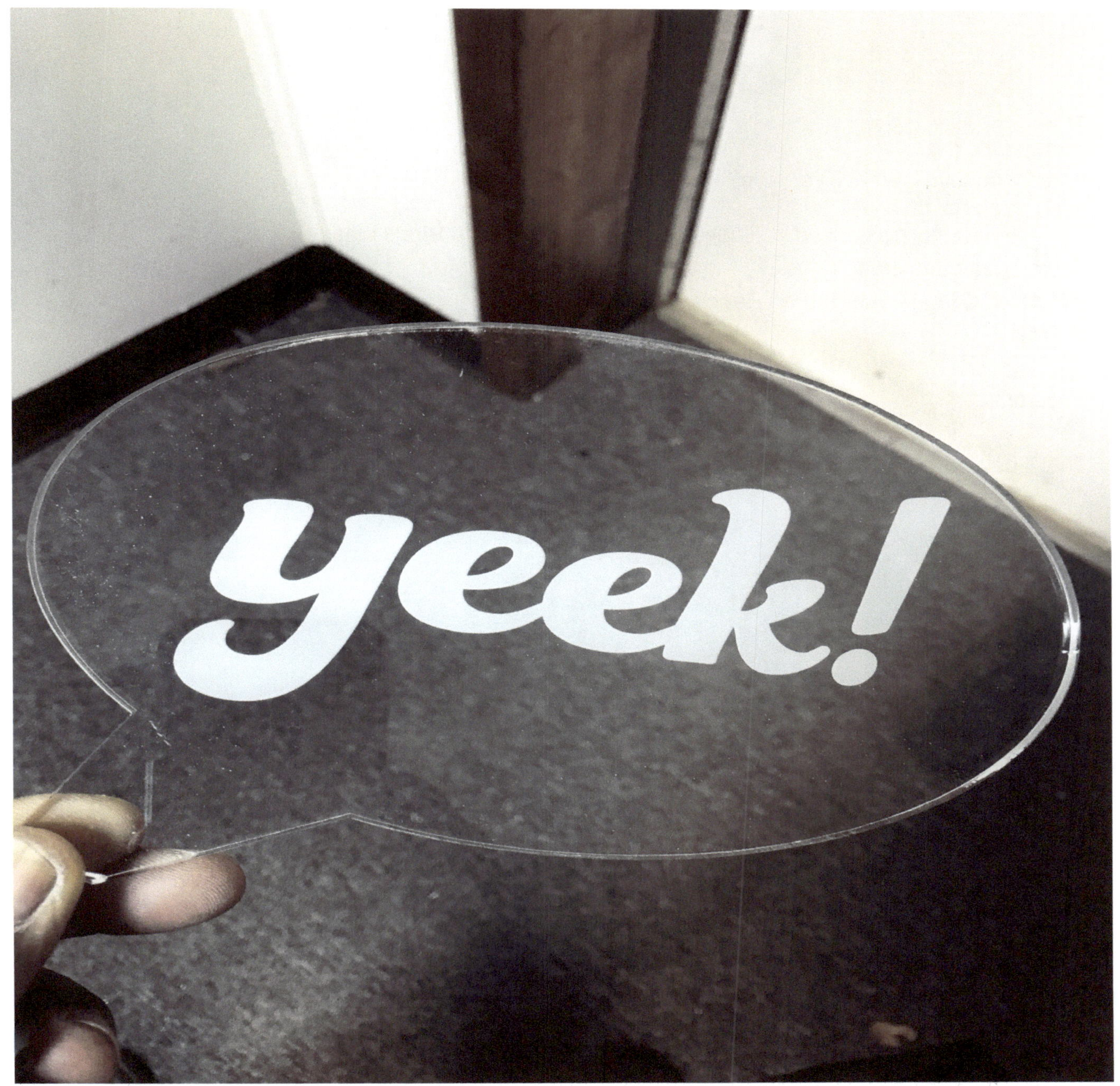
yeek!

The Varsity

What'll ya have? What'll ya have? What'll ya have?

Umm lemme get 1 Glorified, 1 Heavy Dog, and some Onion Rings please
Gotta have them onion rings
A Frosted Orange and a Fried Peach Pie
Oh My!

Call back

That'll be $10.10
Outta Twenty

Ticket # 77
77!!!

Mmmmm
Oooo that Peach Pie

My thighs don't like it but it tastes so good

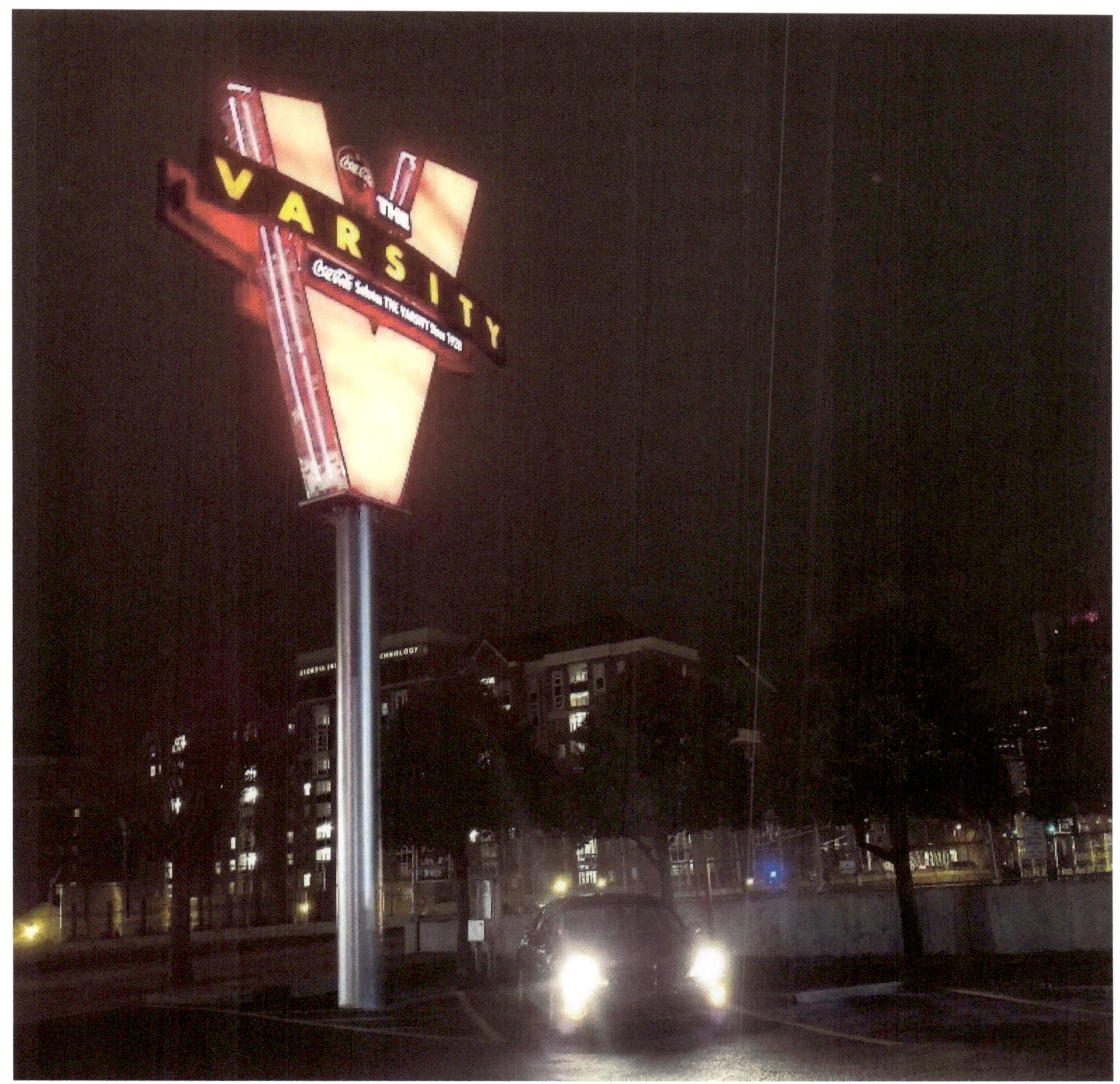
THE
VARSITY

Missing

I remember standing on the playground
with one eye focused on my teacher
and the other on tall dark trees surrounding me

Listening for unfamiliar voices and the sound
of warning whistles
to break the awkward silence of my fear

I sat and watched the face of yet
another child who looked like me
added to the list of bodies found

I now know why my parents would not let
me walk alone even though
I only lived a block away

And to this day, years have passed a mystery
still looms of what was then a time of sheer uncertainty
was it the klan or this black man

A generation scarred, a man who claimed his innocence,
parents with no answers,
the world sorry for our loss, a city lost

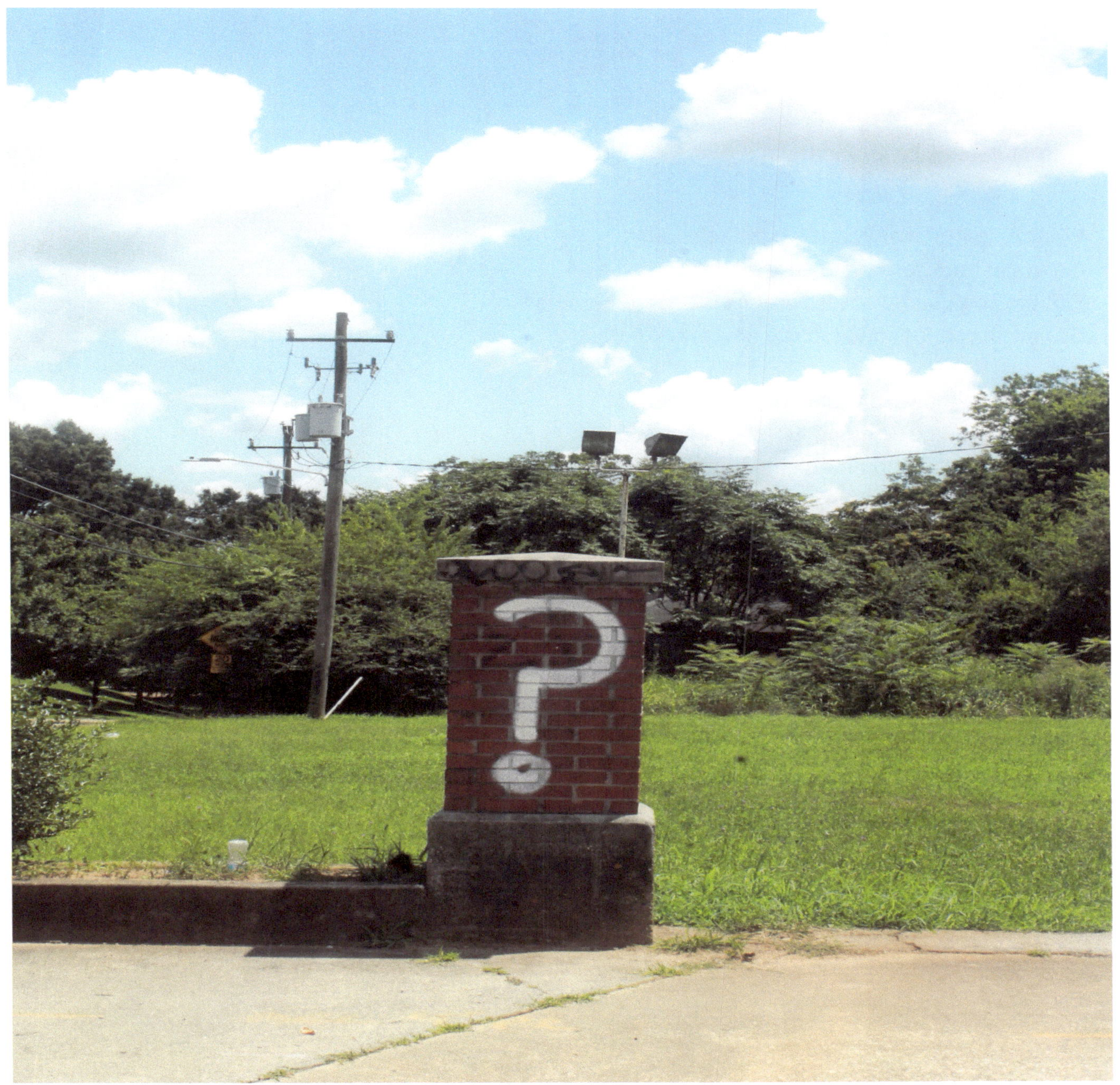

In the Kitchen like Grandma at a Fish Fry

Well I'm going over yonder to the sto house
Gotta get back fore the pastor let the church owt
Finta to cook some collard greens wit some ham hocks
Got my apron, got my doo rag and my red crocs

We got hog maws, skillet corn and ho cakes
Like Shirley say, "U name it!" it's gon get baked
Or battered up in cornmeal and then deep fried
Got chicken legs, wangs, and some peach pies

When I yell for you to come inside from outside
Wash yo hands and then get ready don't be side eyein
Don't ack like you too big for your britches
Or I'll make u go outside and get some switches

Mind ya manners let the ol folks get they plate first
Bow yo head, Bless da food with a Bible verse
I reckon you gon ask me for some drank too
You'll be full as a tick when you get thew

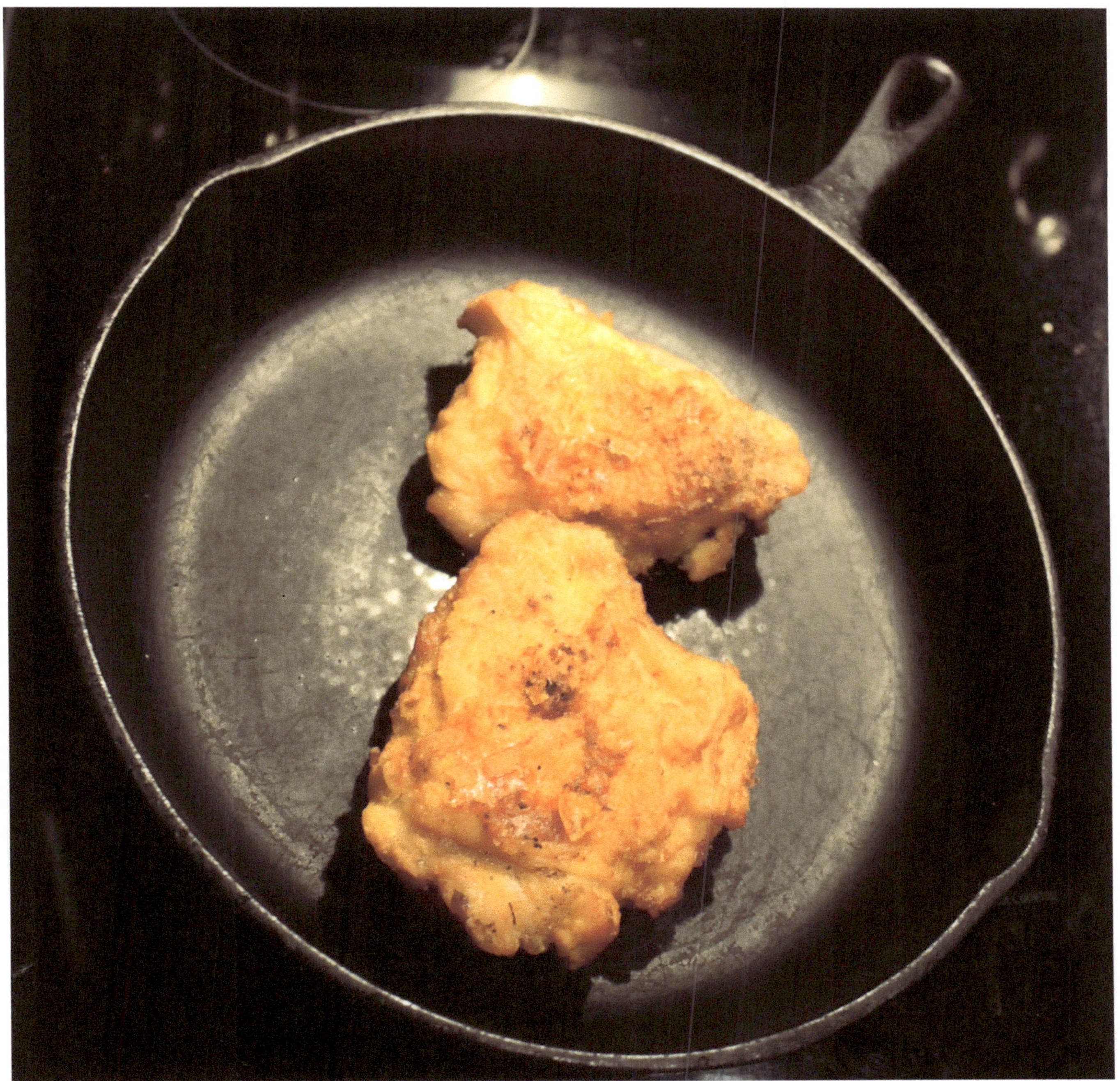

Our Leadership

Maynard was the first Black mayor
A revolutionary

Andrew picked up the baton
and became a visionary

In 1996
Atlanta became international
Hosting the Olympics
Fa sho increased our capital

We were then known as The Centennial City
Then came Mayor Campbell also known as Billy

Shirley became our first lady with flowers o'er her heart
She shattered glass ceilings-played an integral part

Kasim brought the Beltline
and lots of controversy

Now we got Keisha Lance Bottoms
born and raised in the dirty

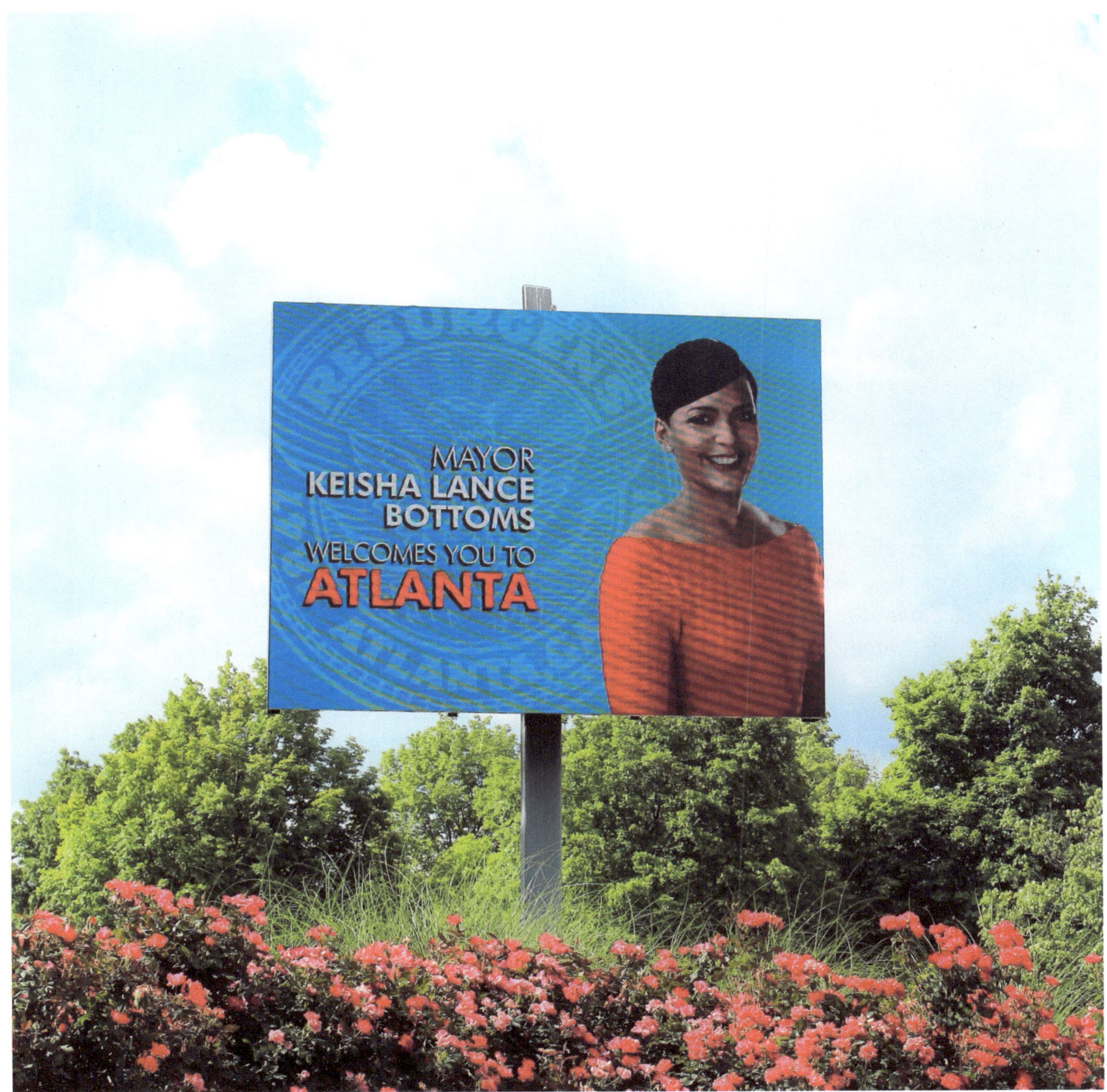
MAYOR
KEISHA LANCE
BOTTOMS
WELCOMES YOU TO
ATLANTA

Southern Belles

Yea we are Southern Belles
but we don't wear big hooped skirts
We rock big hoop earrings
with mid-drift shirts
We gotta a bunch of shawt shawts
maybe eight or nine pair
Cause it's hot as hell here
eleven months out the year

Yea I'm a Southern Belle
twenty-nineteen
I still say please and thank you ma'am
but I can't cook no greens
I drank iced lemonade
with a touch of sweet tea
Baby Scarlet O'Hara
aint got nothing on me

Aint no need for me to lay out
cuz I was born with a tan
I'm an independent woman
I don't lean on no man
And if you piss me off
I aint gon cuss at your azz
I'mma say, "Bless your heart"
and flash a smile as I pass

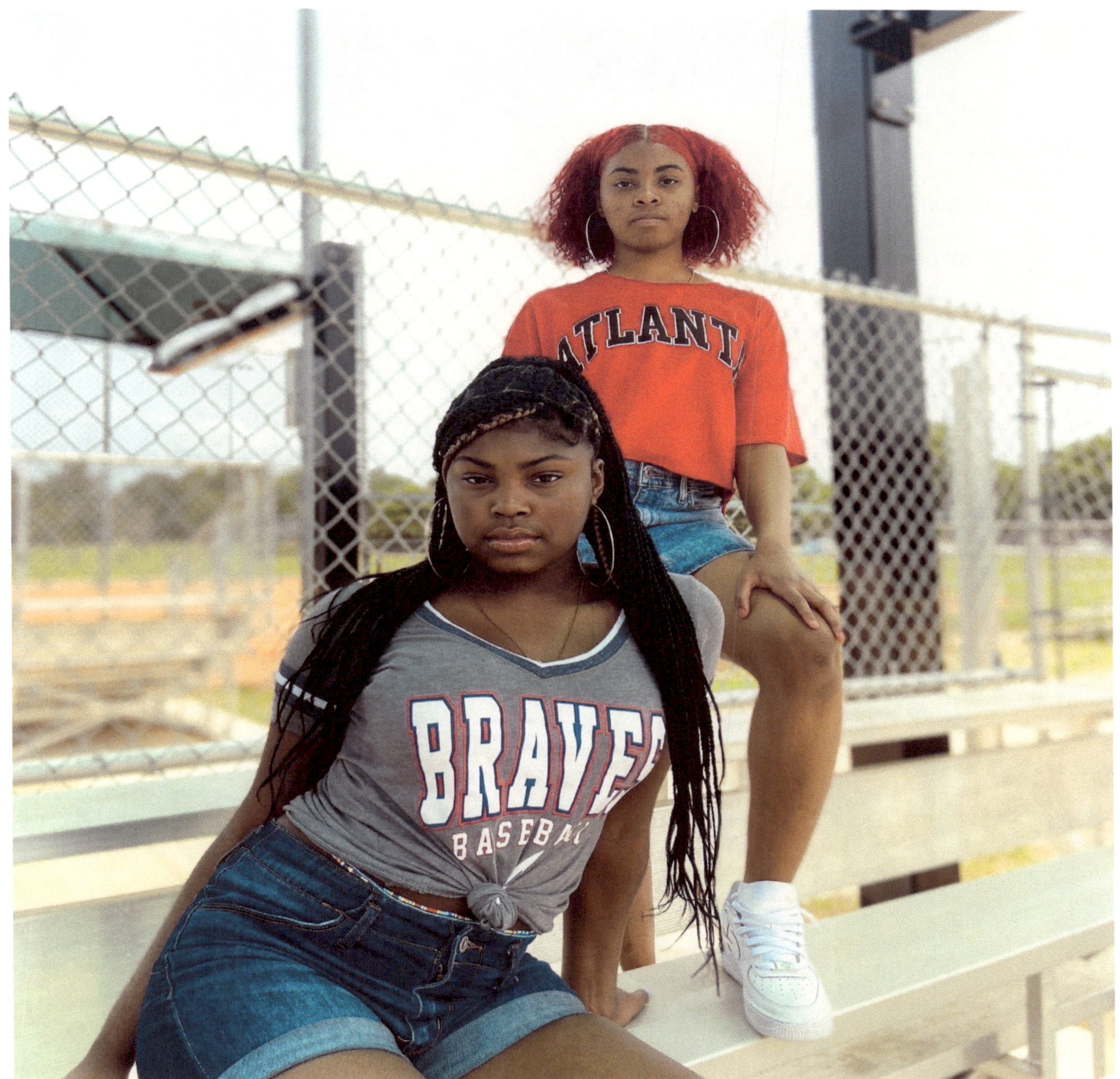

Verification

When you want to know how "@lanta" someone is, you simply need to ask two questions.

1. What hospital were you born in?
2. What high school did you attend?

If you were born at Grady, then you are a REAL Atlanta native. Even though there are many, many, hospitals in the city being a "Grady Baby" gives you ATLien street credit.
If you attended high school at an Atlanta Public School you also get points. Even if you went to school in Decatur where its greater or East Point College Park you will be respected but don't try to claim to be from the ATL and you if graduated from Pebblebrook or Parkview…Boo you aint nowhere near Native.

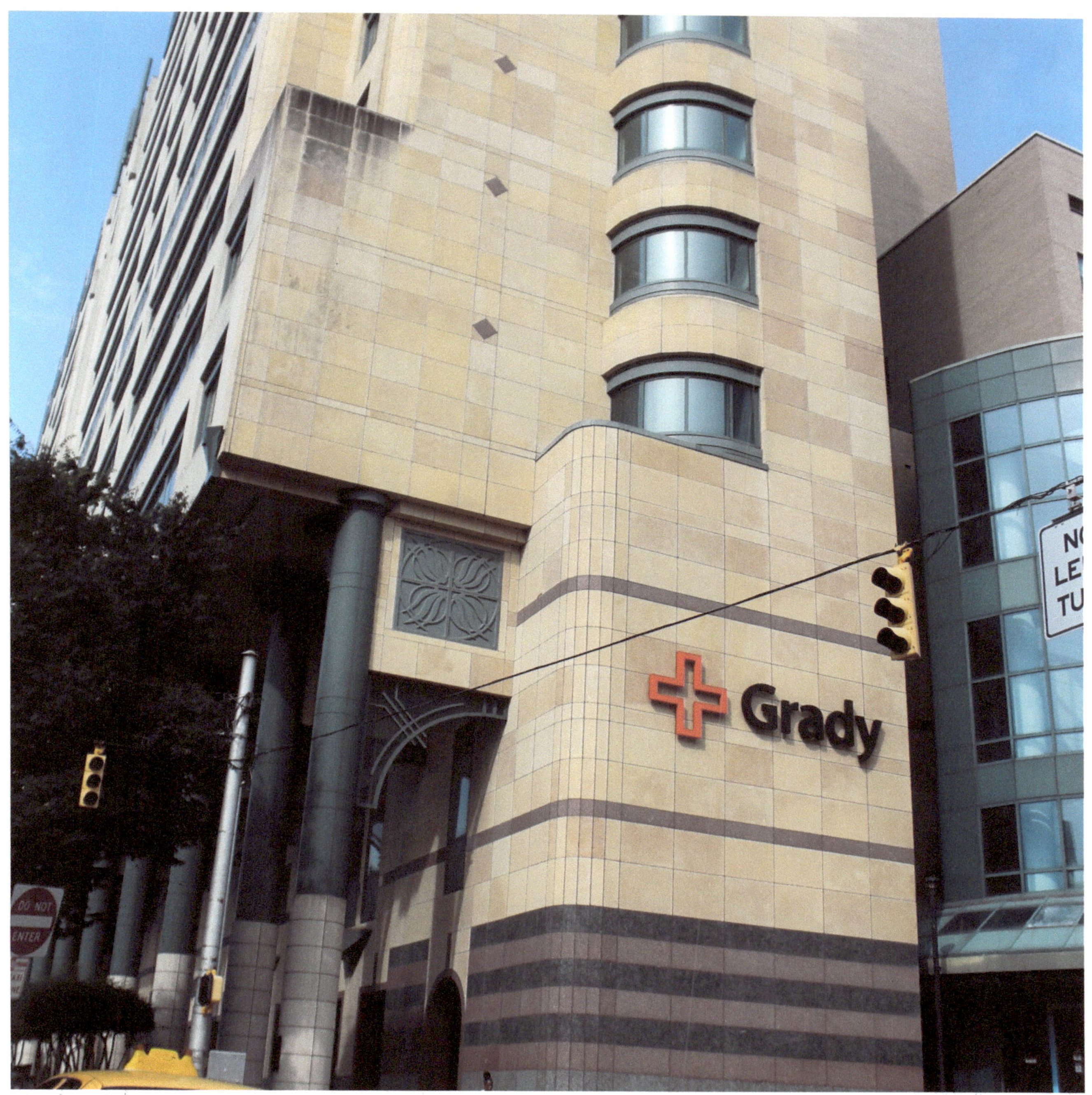
Grady
DO NOT
ENTER

Worlds Biggest Fan

Fanatic Fan
Pride for your team
Faithfully in the stands at every game
Win Lose or Tie
A devoted fan until u die
Logo tattooed on your arm
Forever inked to show the world
You love your team with all your heart
Passionate focused
A supporter
More than a hat, a shirt, a sticker on your cheek
more than a ticket to the super bowl
Will always defend the quarterback and coaches
No matter the play
Nalia in the car representing on the road
A whole room of treasures in the home that you own
if you could be a cheerleader
the crowd would hear your voice over all the others
Dirty Birds will forever fly high in your eyes

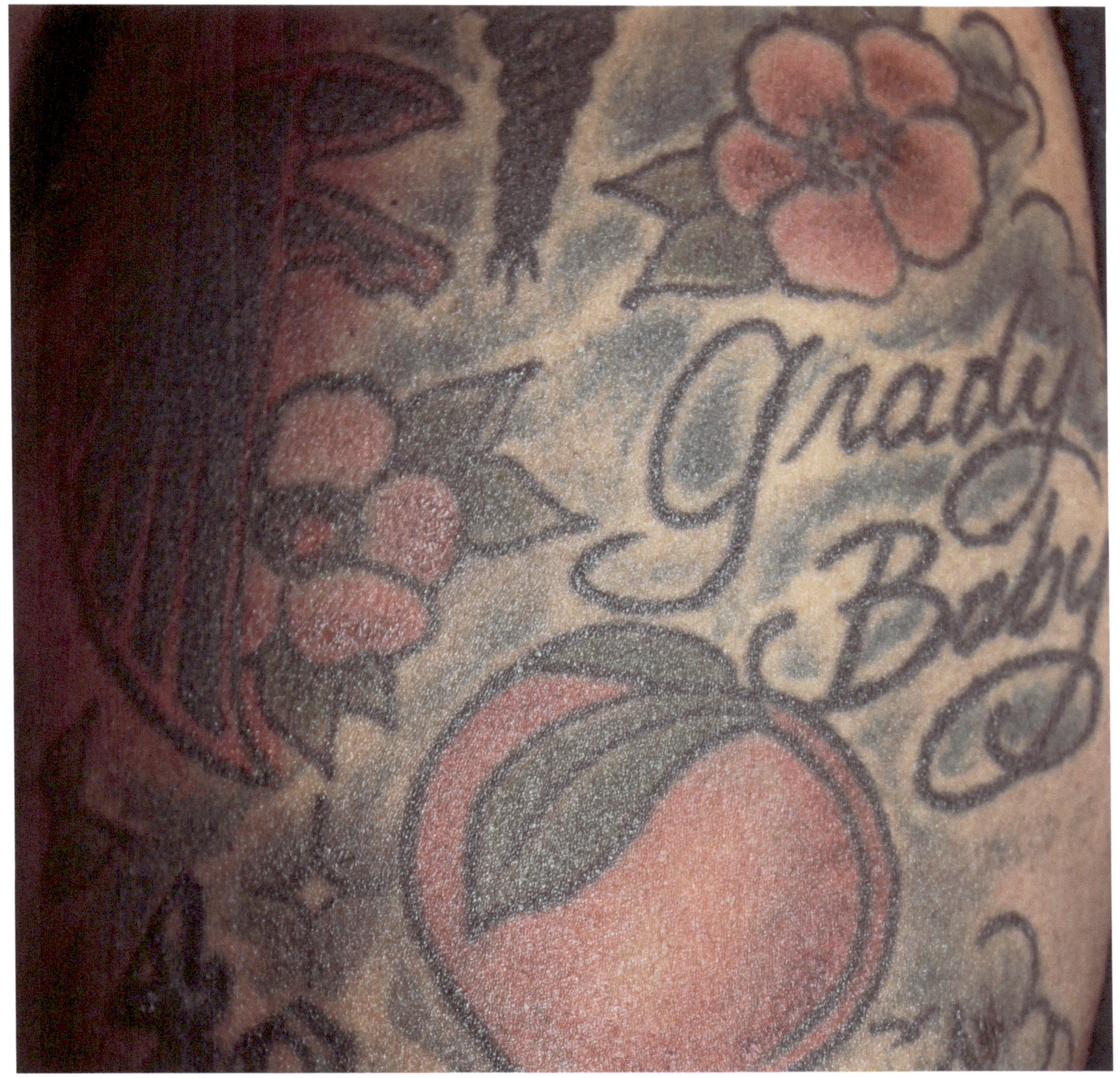

Red Clay

you can’t walk on Georgia Red Clay with chucks on in the summer
cause the dust that comes from the dirt you kick up
as you strolling down the lane
will most certainly leave a stain

you can’t drive on Georgia Red Clay at all in the spring
cause the rain that fell last week will turn your driveway into
muddy pools of stagnant water
that will turn your pickup terra cotta

you can’t play on Georgia Red Clay while its cold in the winter
cause when we get that record two inches of snow
the snowman you build I suppose
will match the color of his carrot nose

the only time you are allowed to enjoy Georgia Clay is in the Fall
cause that is when the leaves rain down from mighty oaks and maples
and the clay adhere the leaves unto the street
that transform them into gold beneath my feet

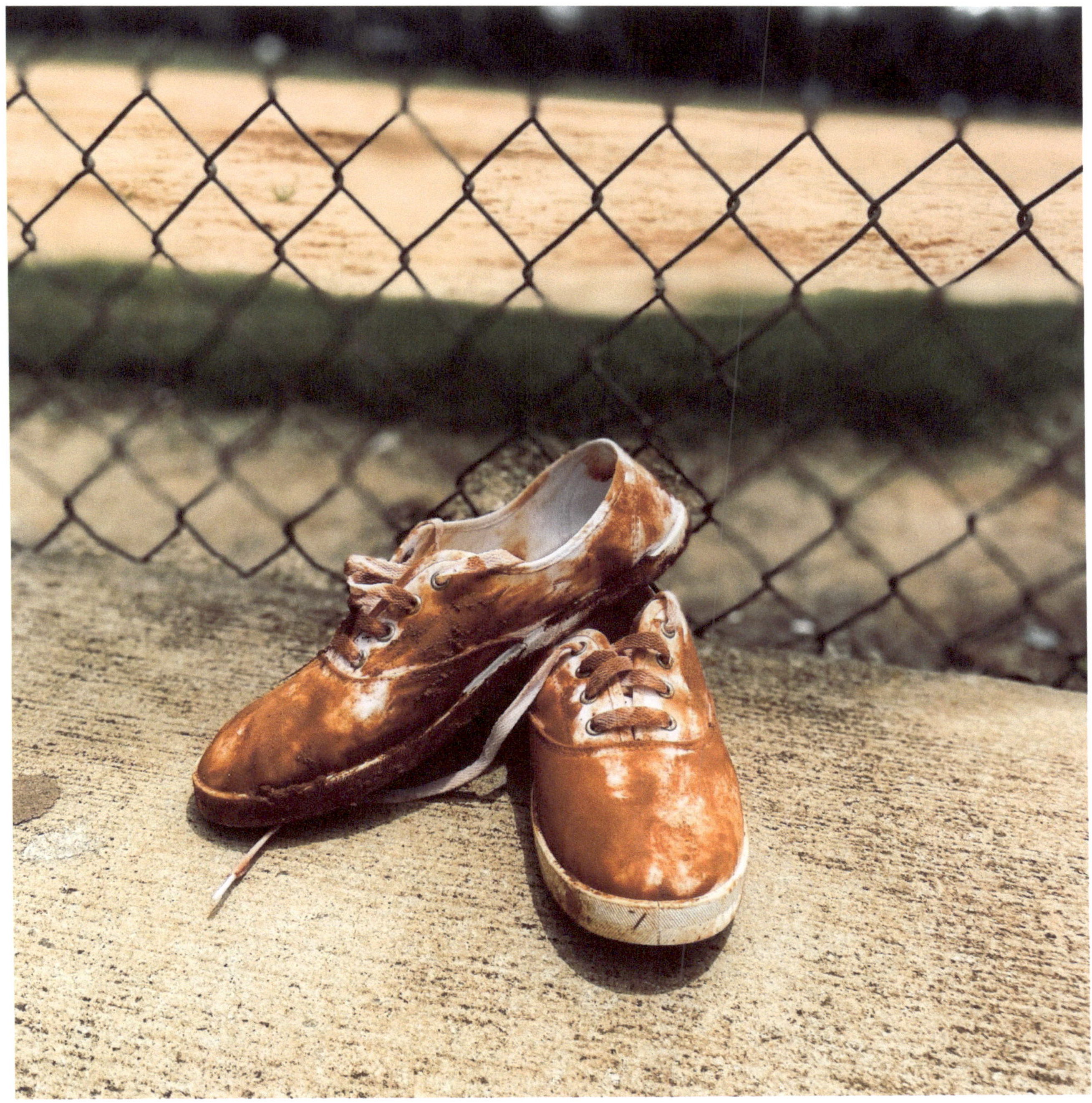

black@lanta

black@lanta is where I stay
I got a black attitude
every black azz day

I drive a big black benz
with big black tires
On black asphalt
through the hood I ride

I got black people problems and black folk bills
I got high blood pressure take 3,4 pills

I'm always fighting
got 2 black eyes
Trying to keep my neighborhood vitalized

Trying to teach my black son how to survive
Trying to help my black girls realize

That they are beautiful queens
no matter what they size
and we black@lanta proud
til de day that we die

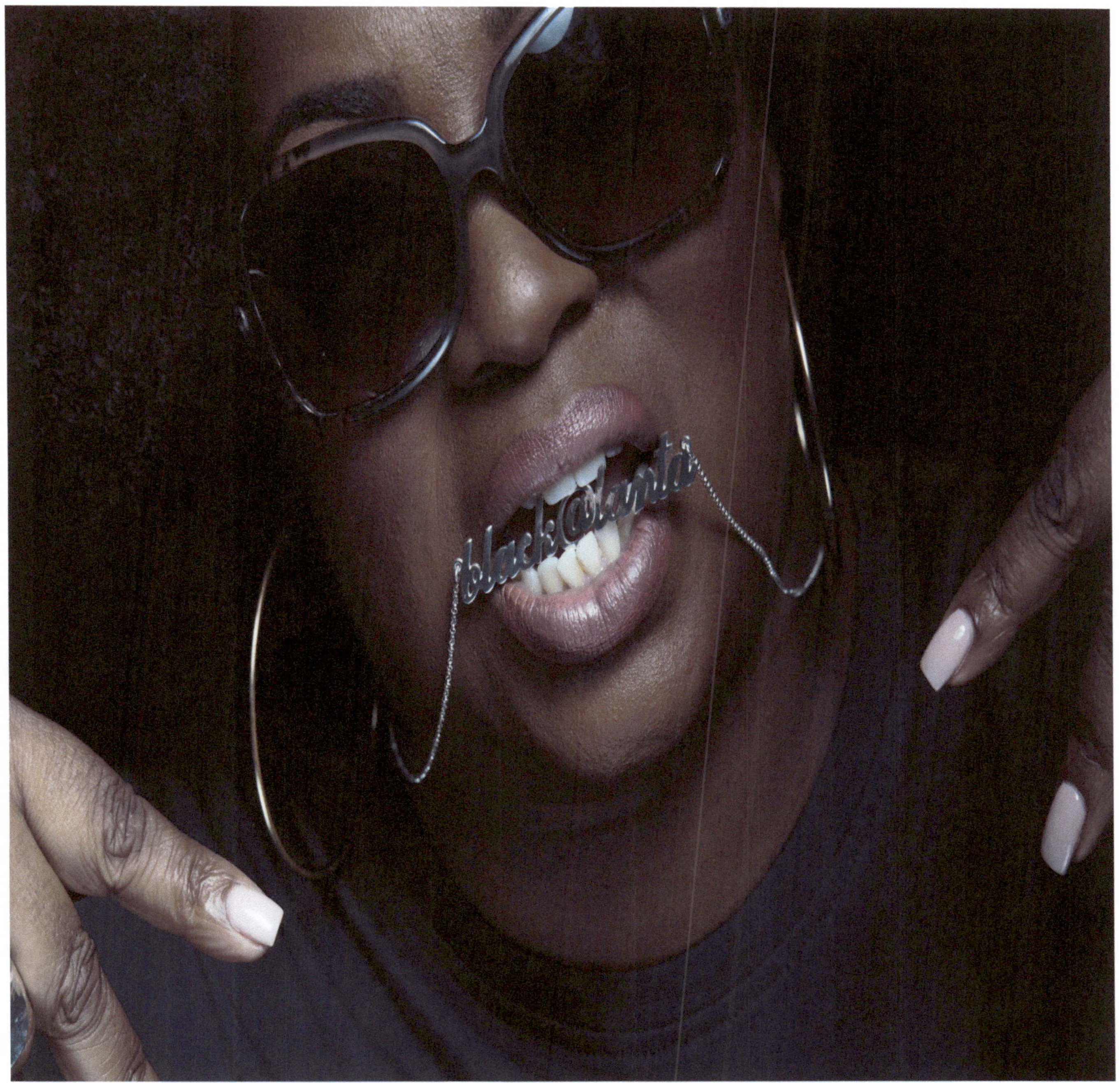
black@lanta

G.R.I.T.S. vs B.I.S.C.U.I.T.S.

Grits are white
and usually salty
You gotta throw em in hot water
for them to even have flavor
Corny to say the least

Biscuits on the other hand
are soft and brown and round
usually served with honey, jam or jelly
sweet like pie
a hardy addition to any meal

Black Intellectual Sisters Cultivated Uniquely in this Southernheat

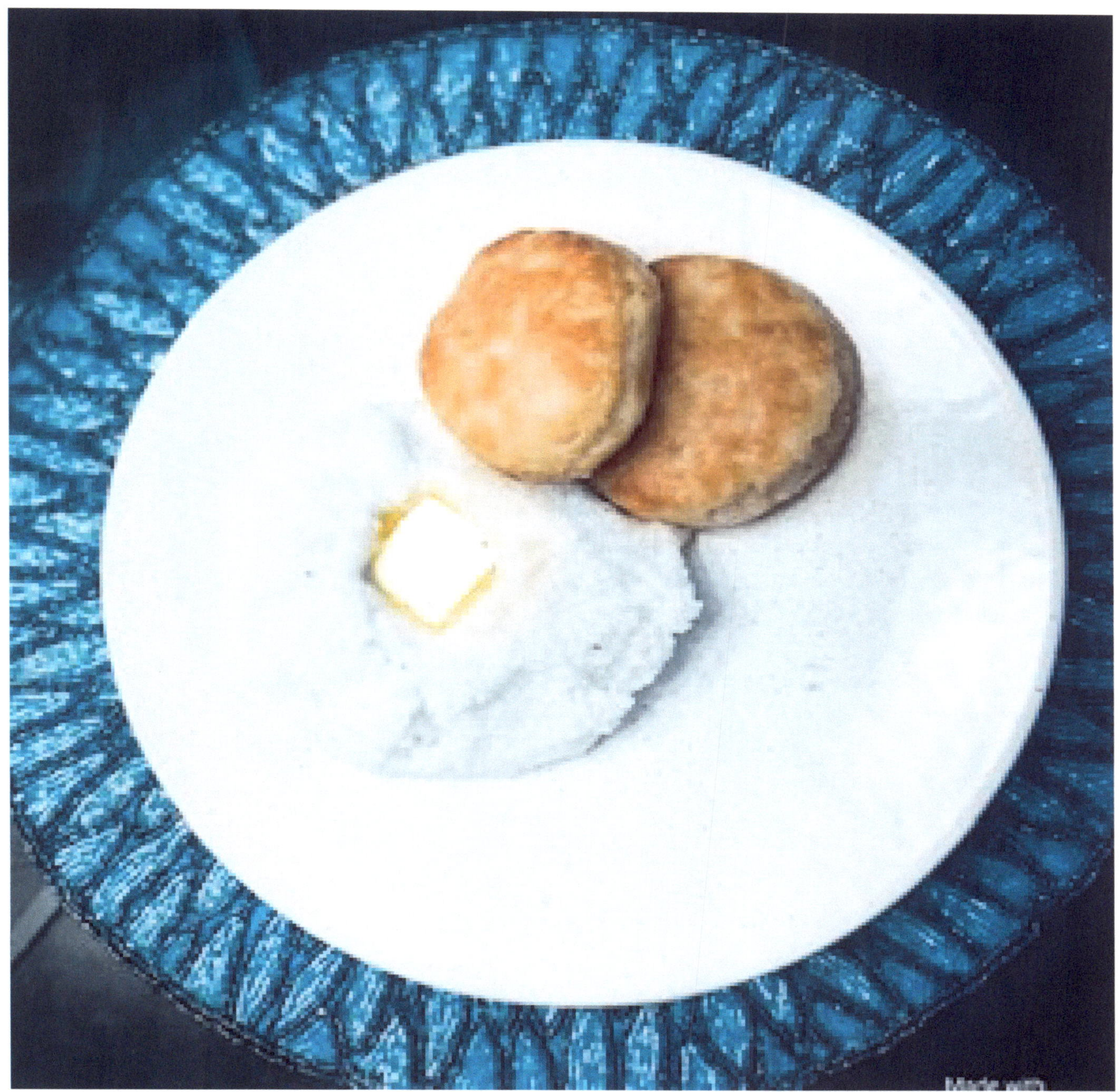
Made with

marta's smarter

Officially known as the Metropolitan Atlanta Rapid Transit Authority
Unofficially Moving African Americans Rapidly through Atlanta, really?

I bet if I asked 10 people what does m.a.r.t.a. stand for they would not know
It is a method of transportation the way people get to and fro
Buses and trains but not like New York or Chicago
Very limited in where it can go in the Metro

Some cities don't want marta in their neighborhoods
They're afraid that colored folks will have access to their goods

When's the last time you saw a thief on the bus with a television set
Amber Alert sends license plate numbers in my text
I wished more people would use marta cuz traffic is a mess
Folks having melt downs on I-20 cause they stressed

Blue Yellow Orange colors of the sky
marta's smarter
take it
when you don't wanna drive

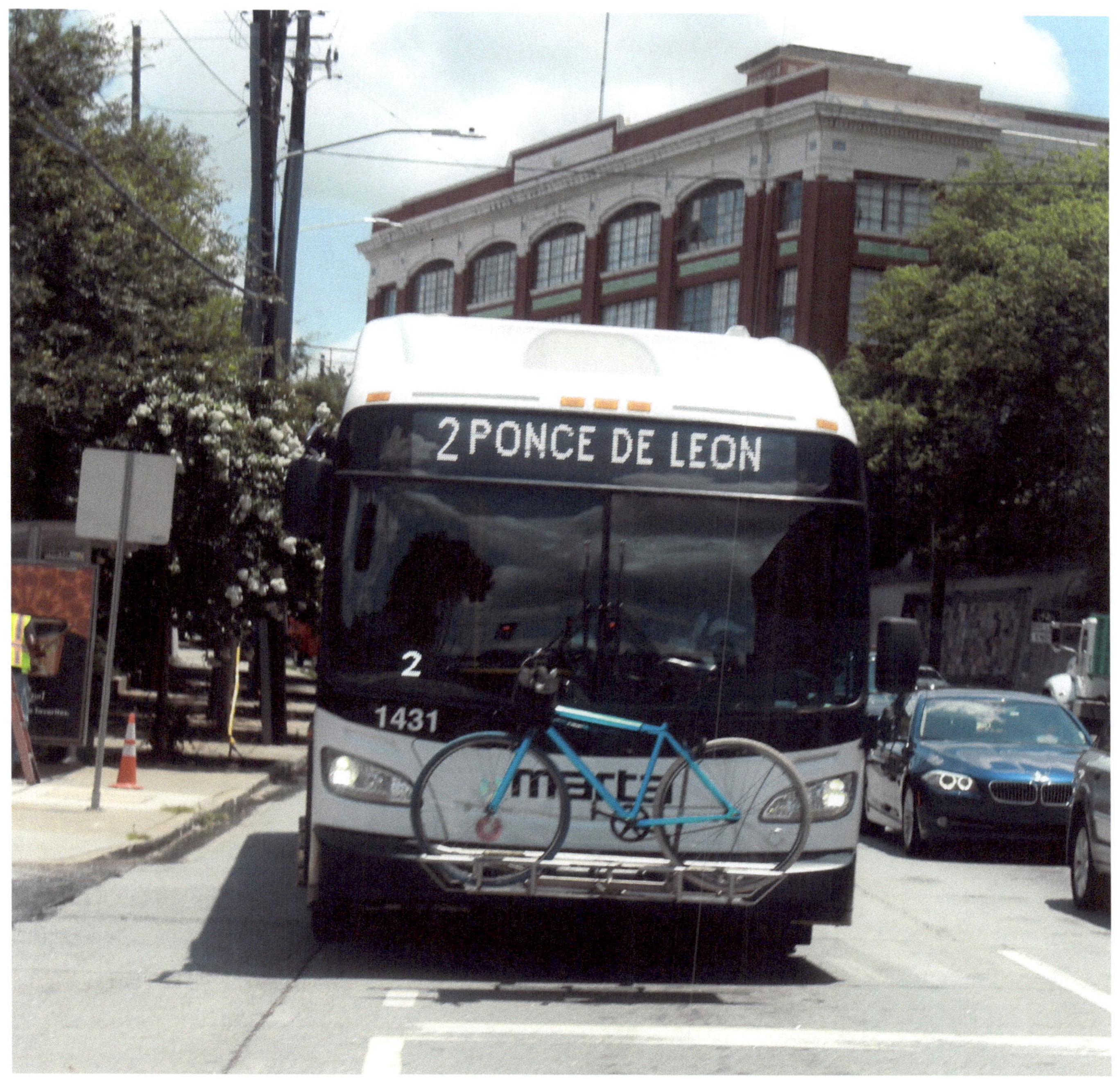
2 PONCE DE LEON
2
1431
marta

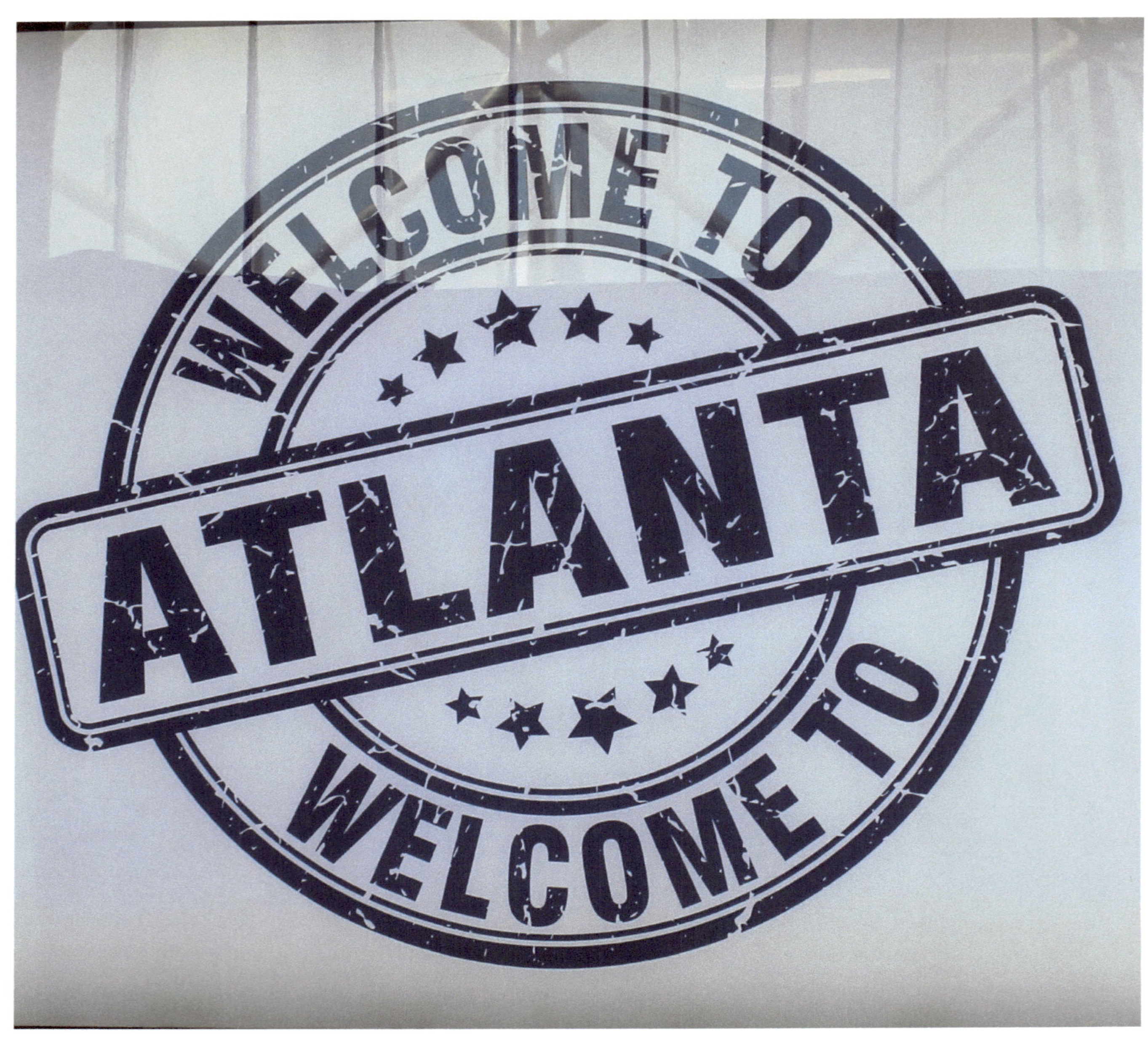
WELCOME TO
ATLANTA
WELCOME TO

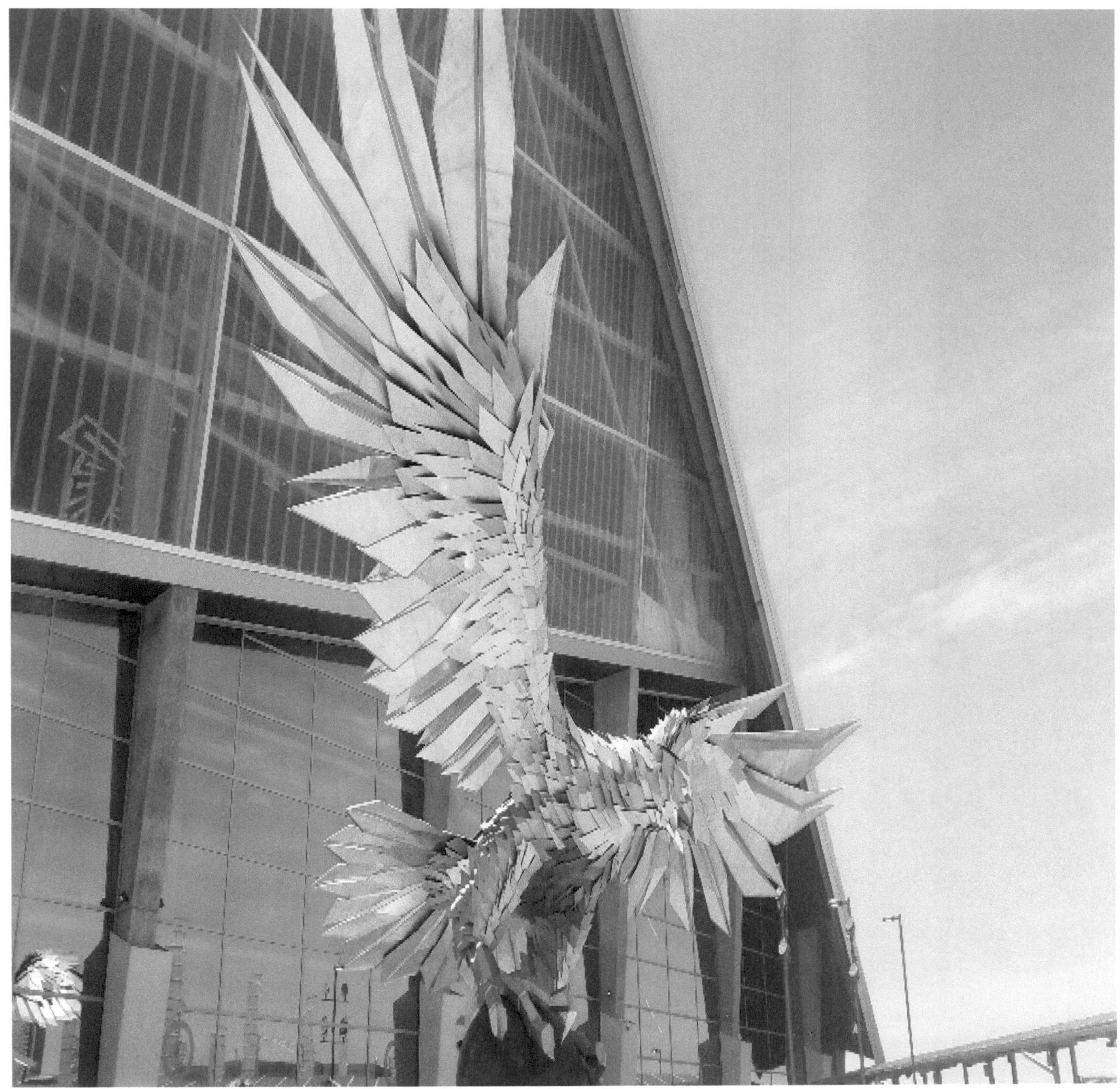

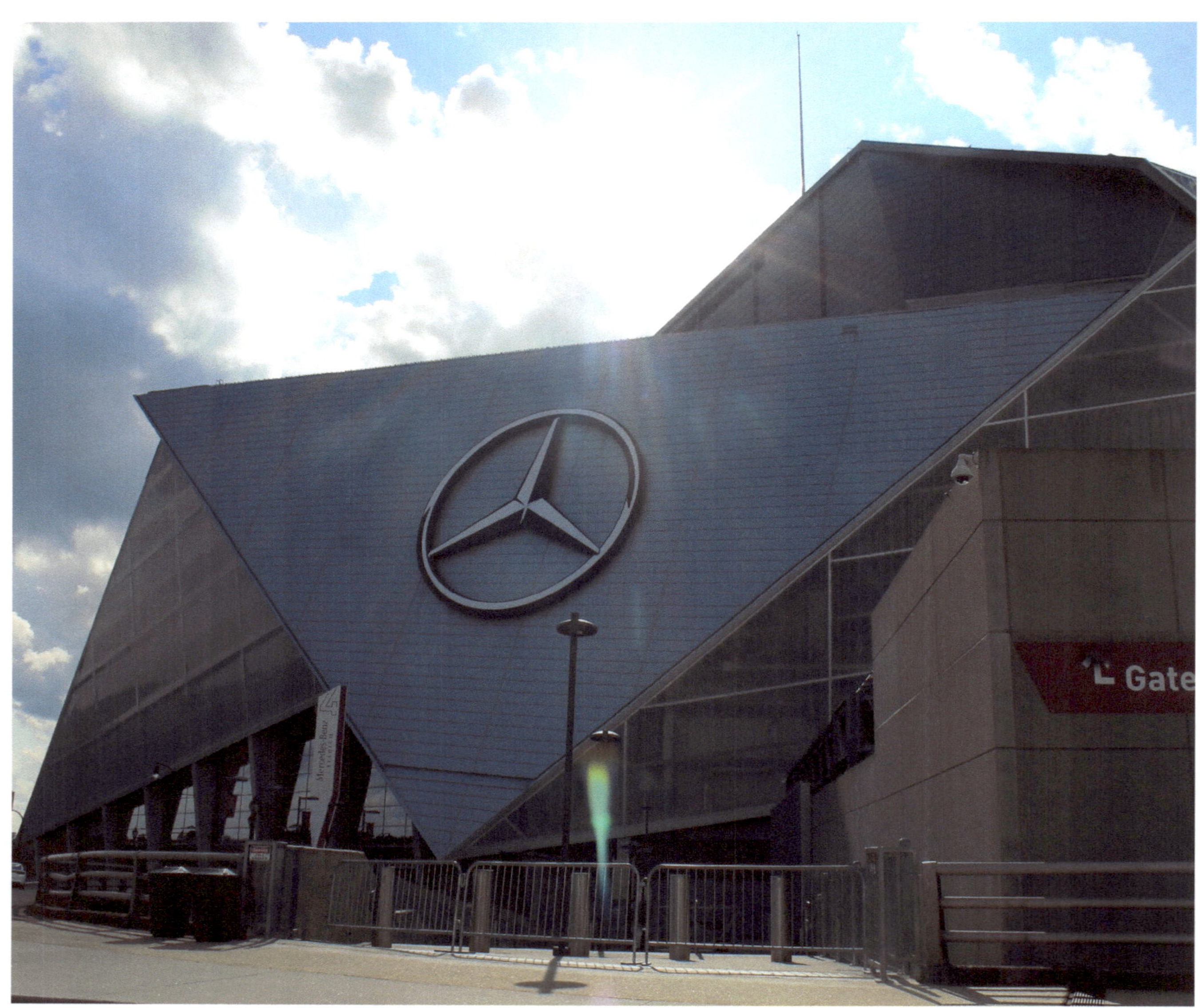
Gate

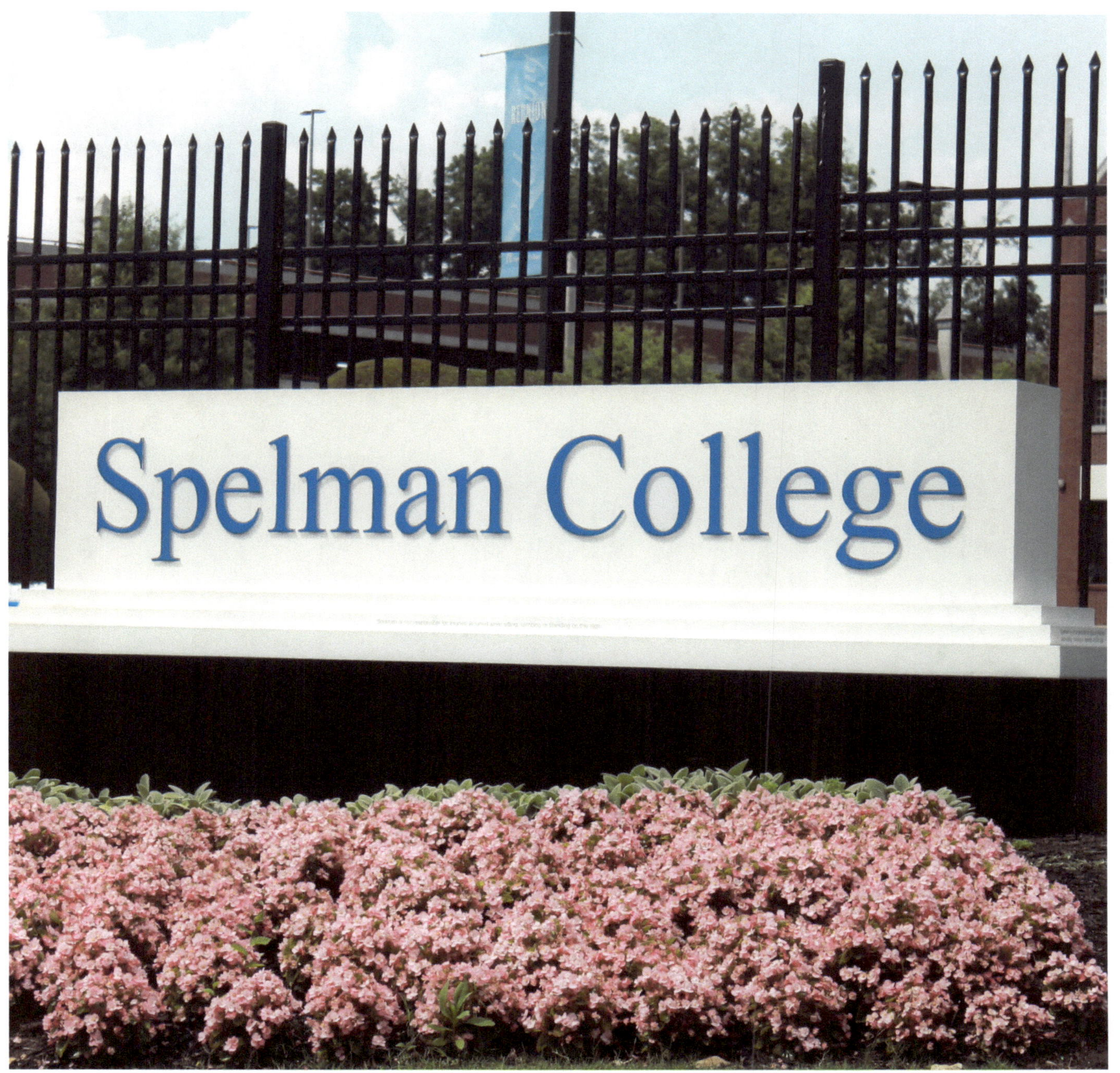
Spelman College

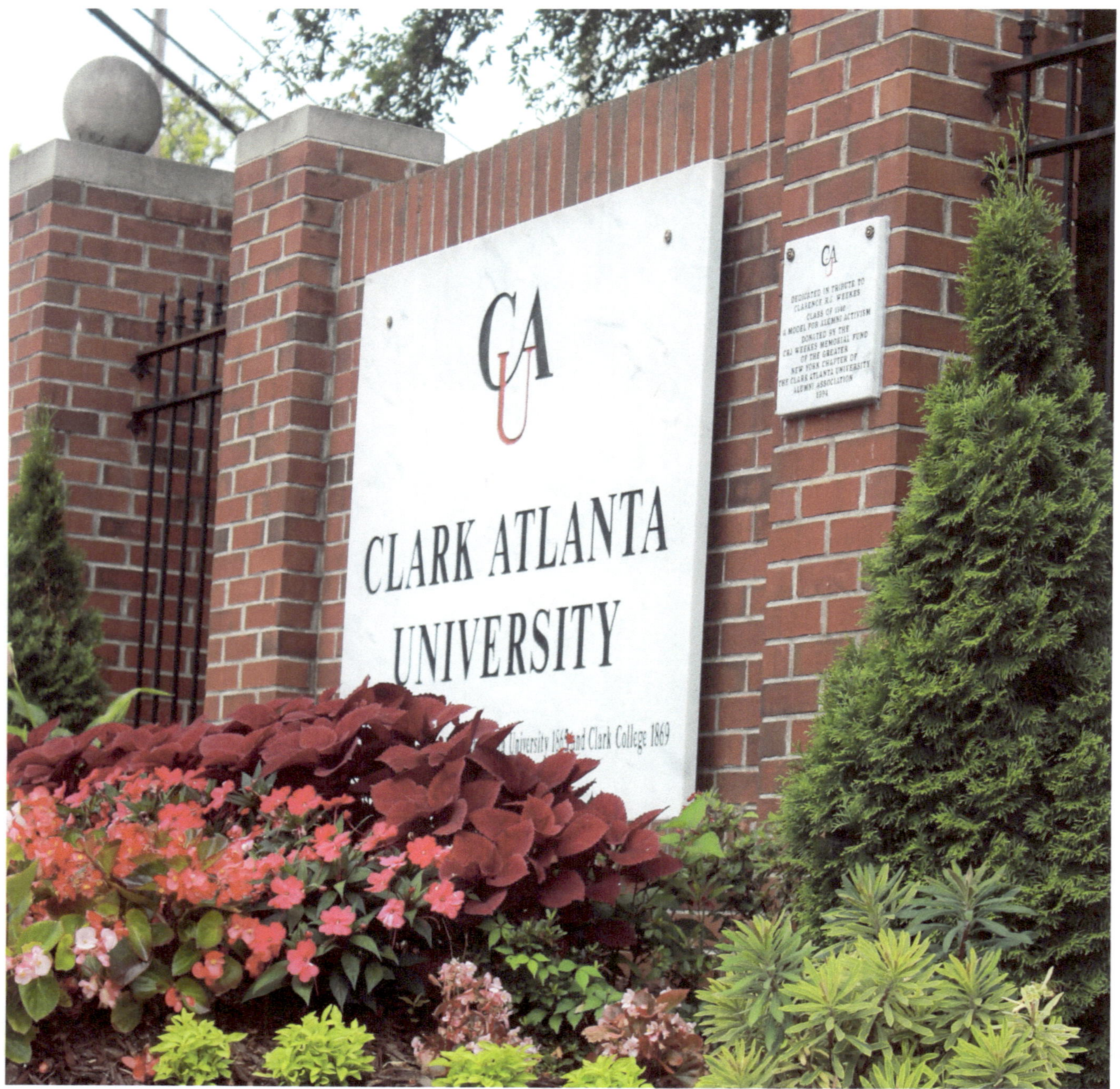
CAU
CLARK ATLANTA
UNIVERSITY
and Clark College 1869
CAU
DEDICATED IN TRIBUTE TO
A MODEL FOR ALUMNI ACTIVISM
DONATED BY THE
OF THE GREATER
NEW YORK CHAPTER OF
THE CLARK ATLANTA UNIVERSITY
ALUMNI ASSOCIATION

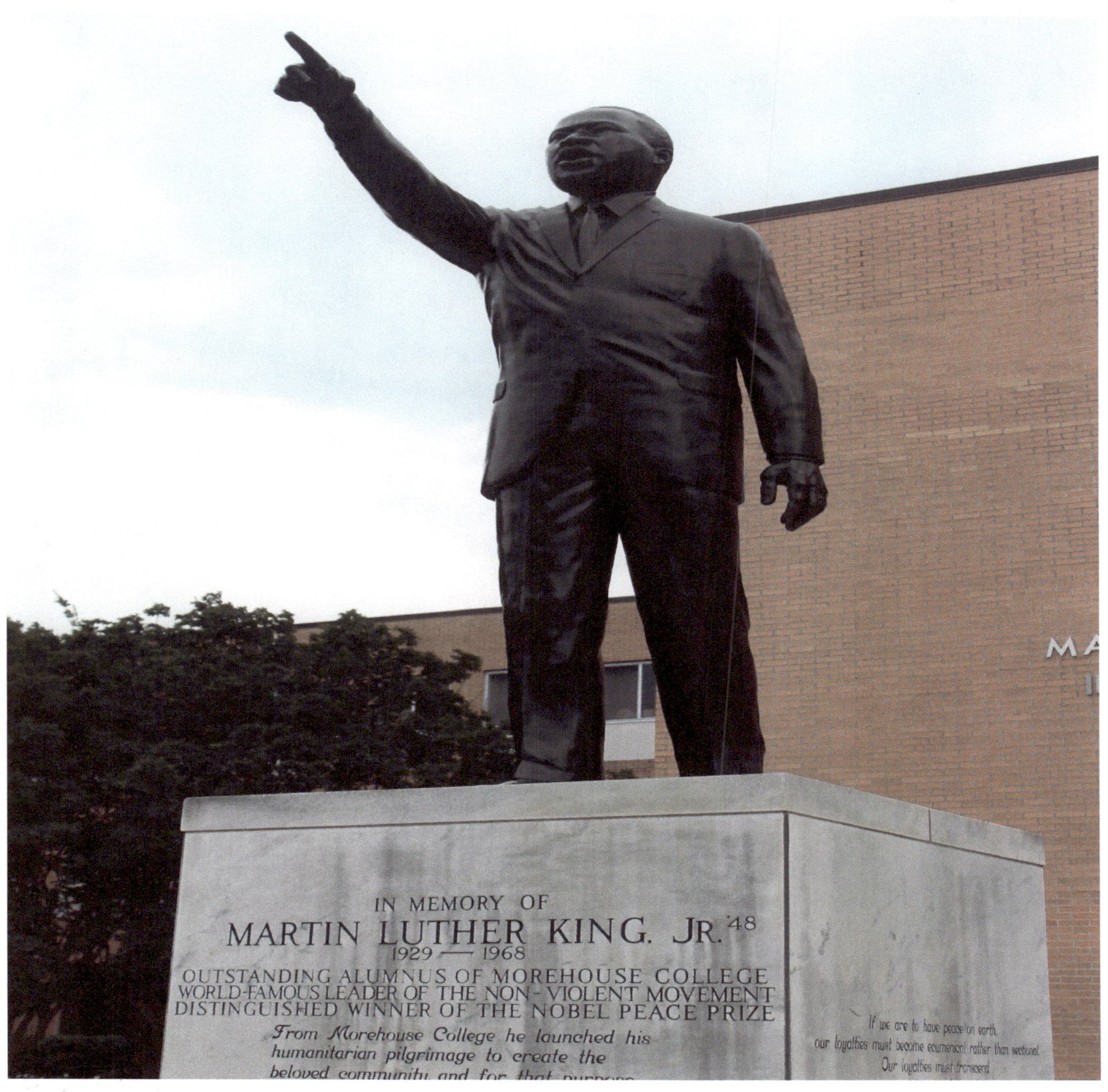
IN MEMORY OF
MARTIN LUTHER KING. JR. '48
1929 — 1968
OUTSTANDING ALUMNUS OF MOREHOUSE COLLEGE
WORLD-FAMOUS LEADER OF THE NON-VIOLENT MOVEMENT
DISTINGUISHED WINNER OF THE NOBEL PEACE PRIZE
From Morehouse College he launched his
humanitarian pilgrimage to create the
If we are to have peace on earth,
our loyalties must become ecumenical rather than sectional.
Our loyalties must transcend

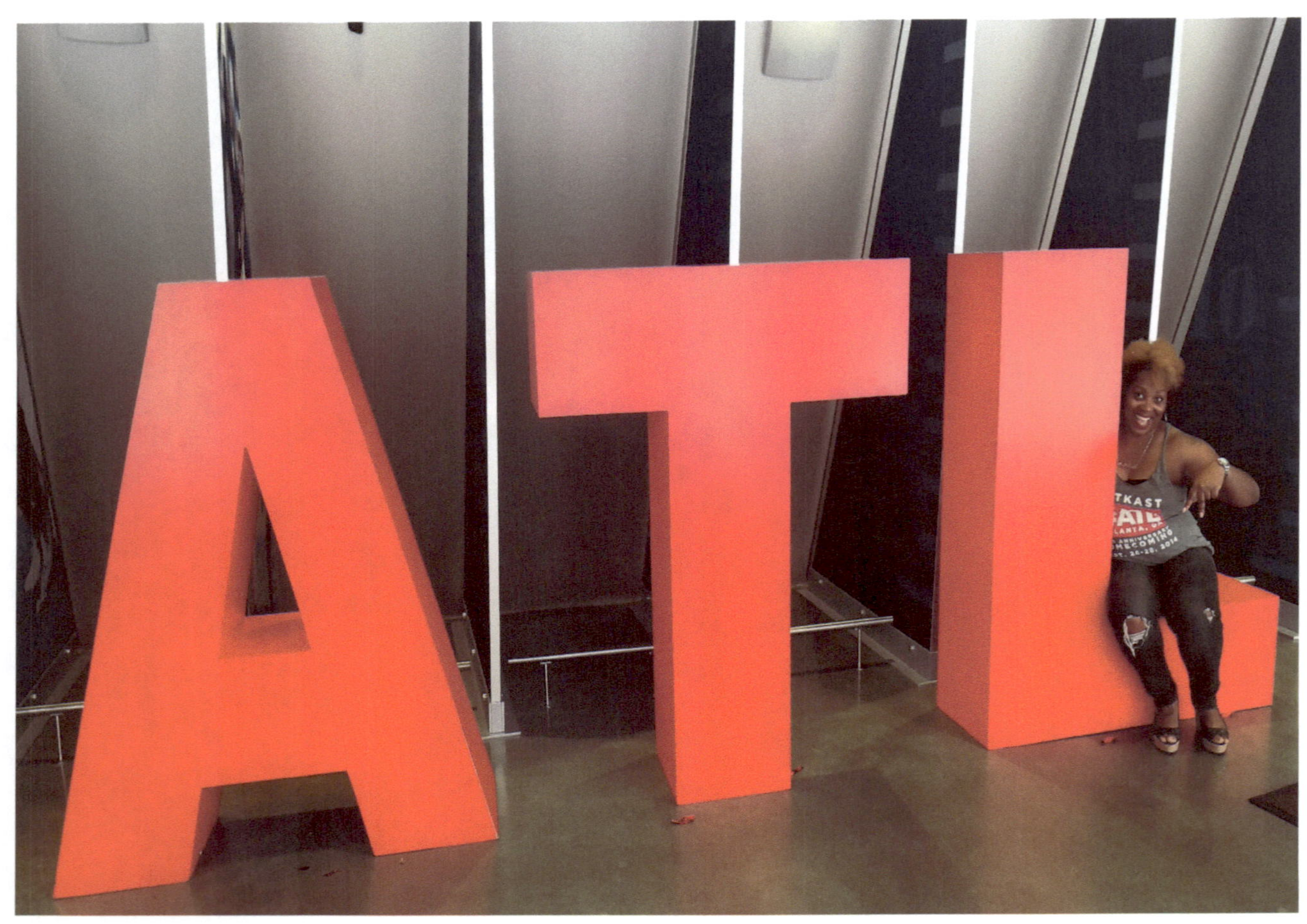
ATL

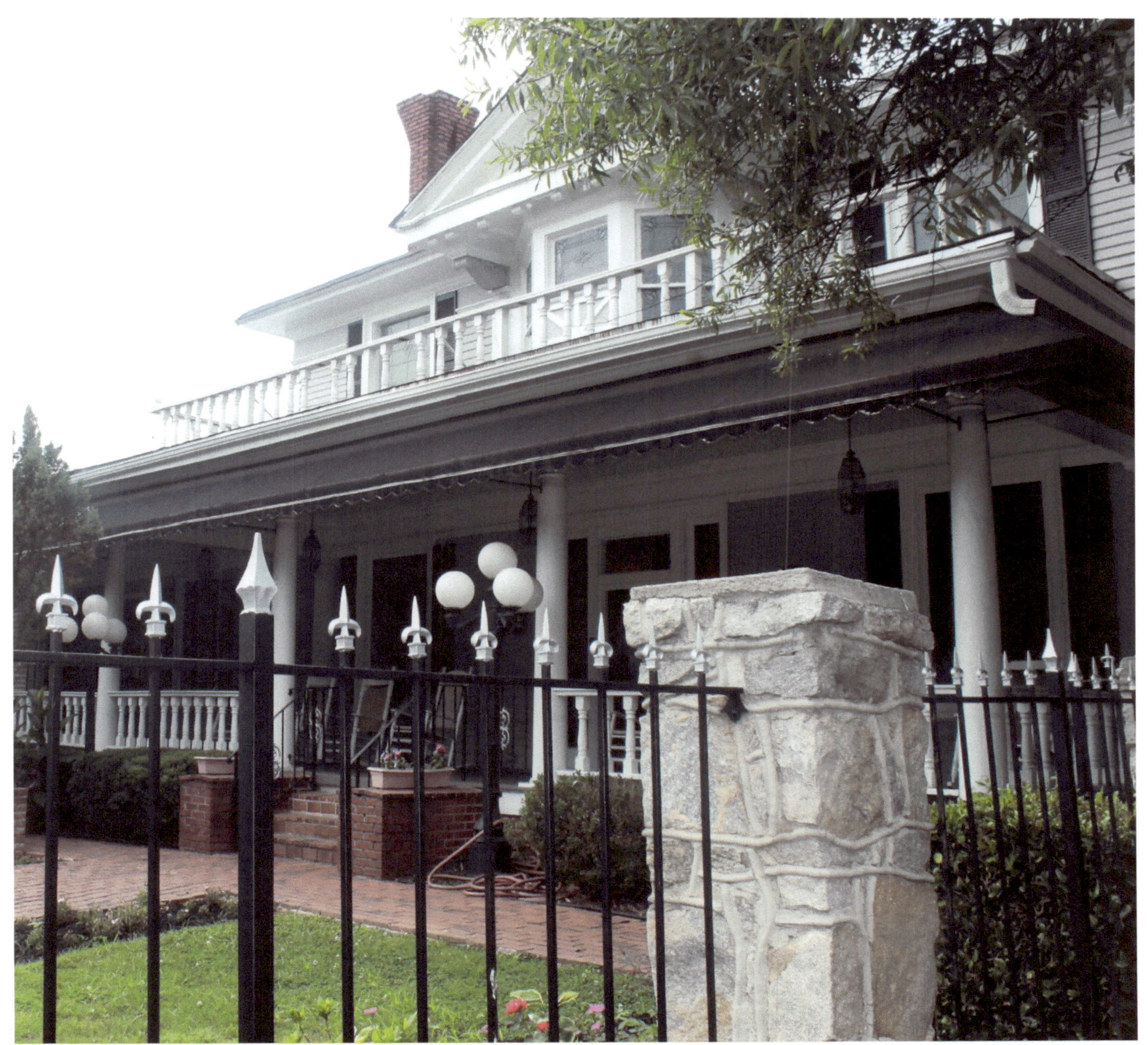

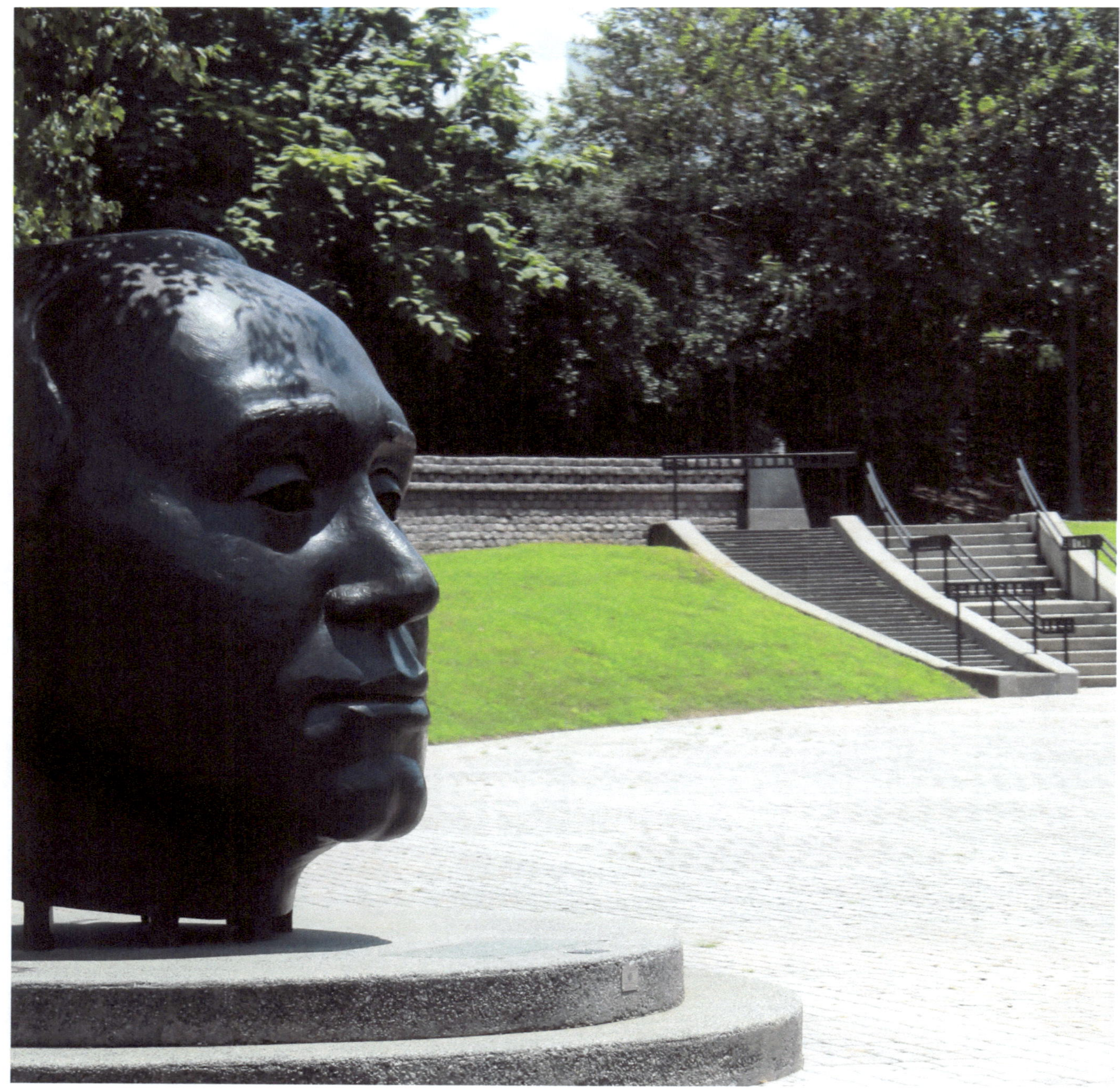

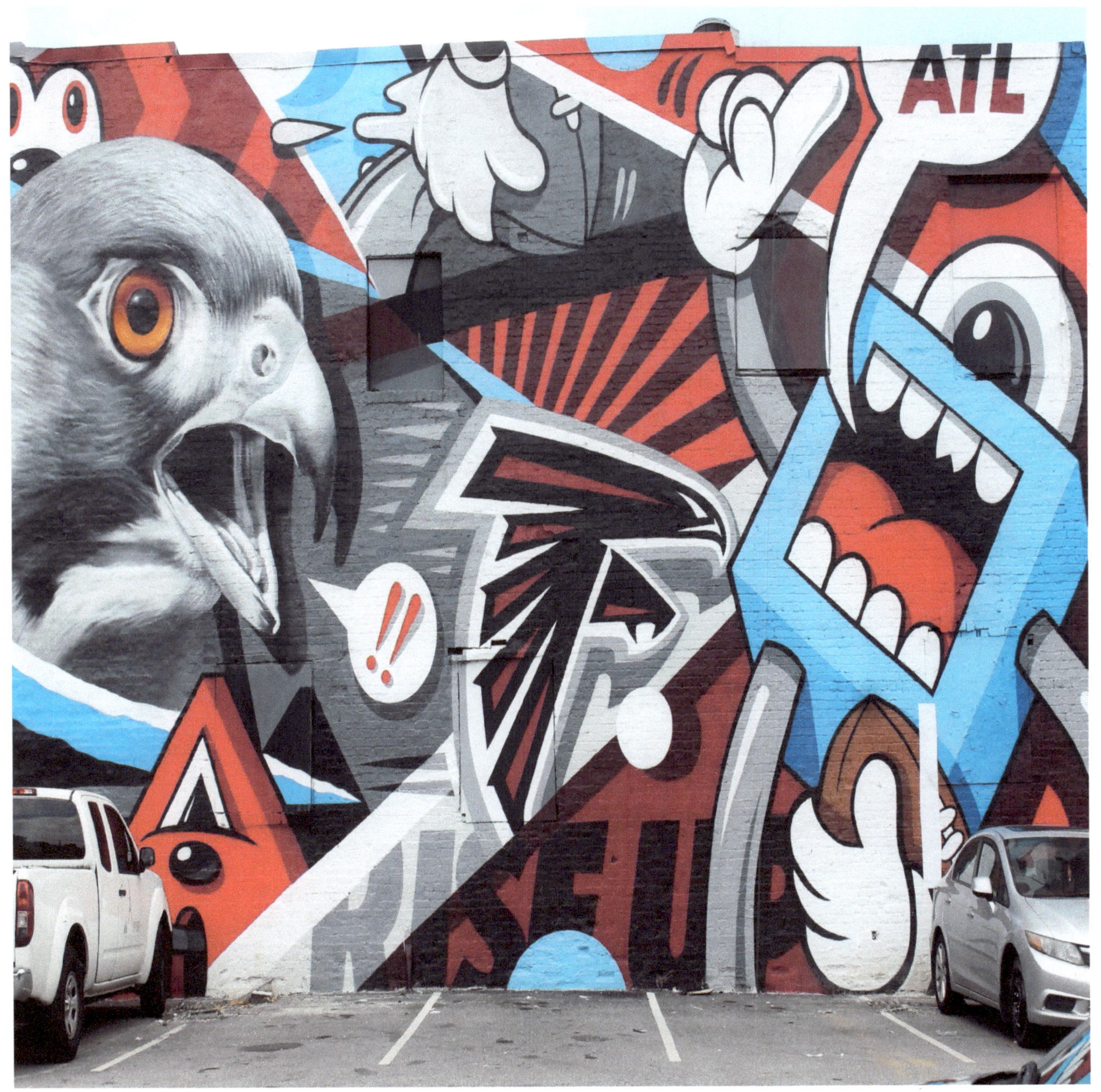
ATL

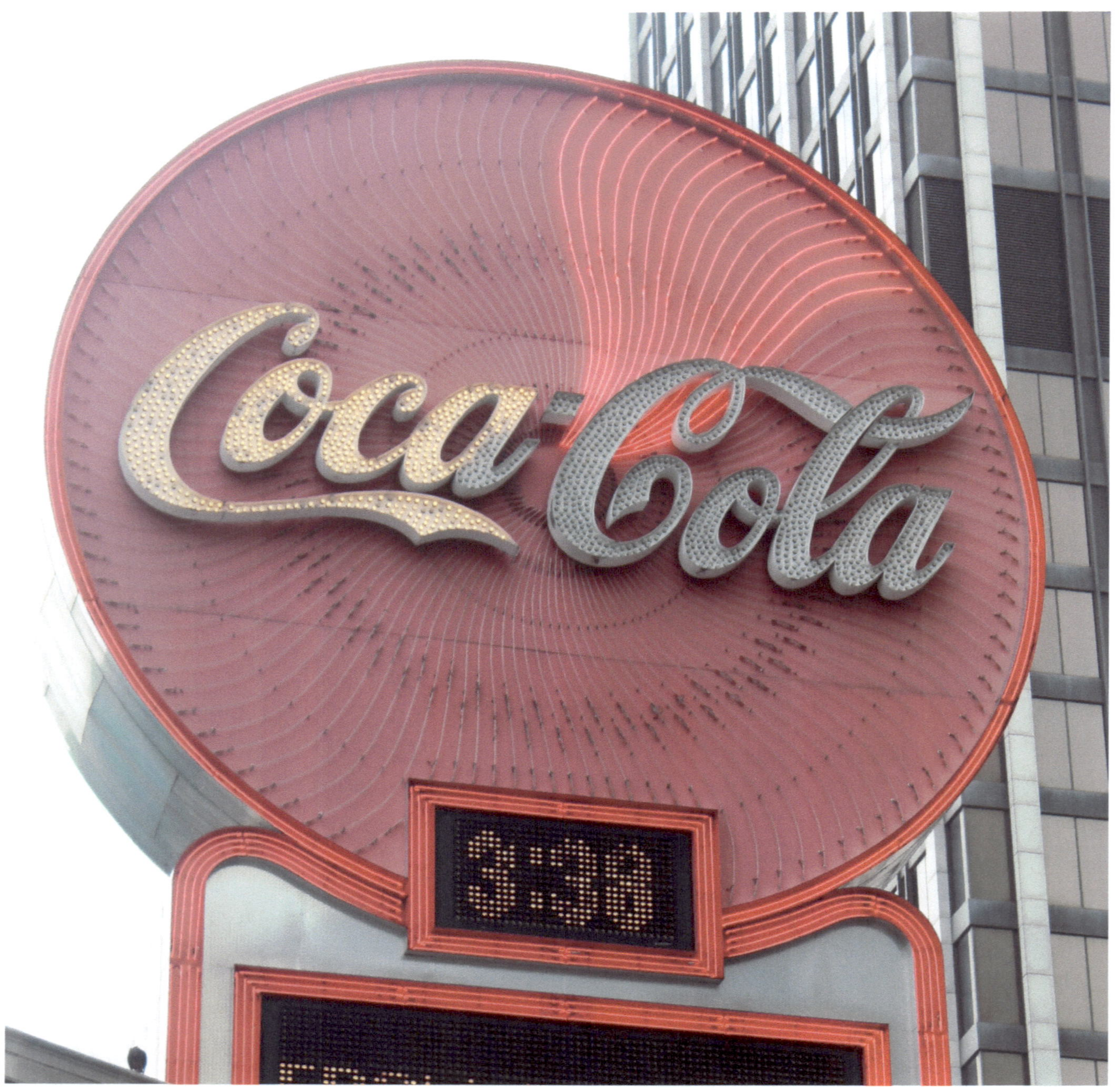
Coca-Cola
3:38

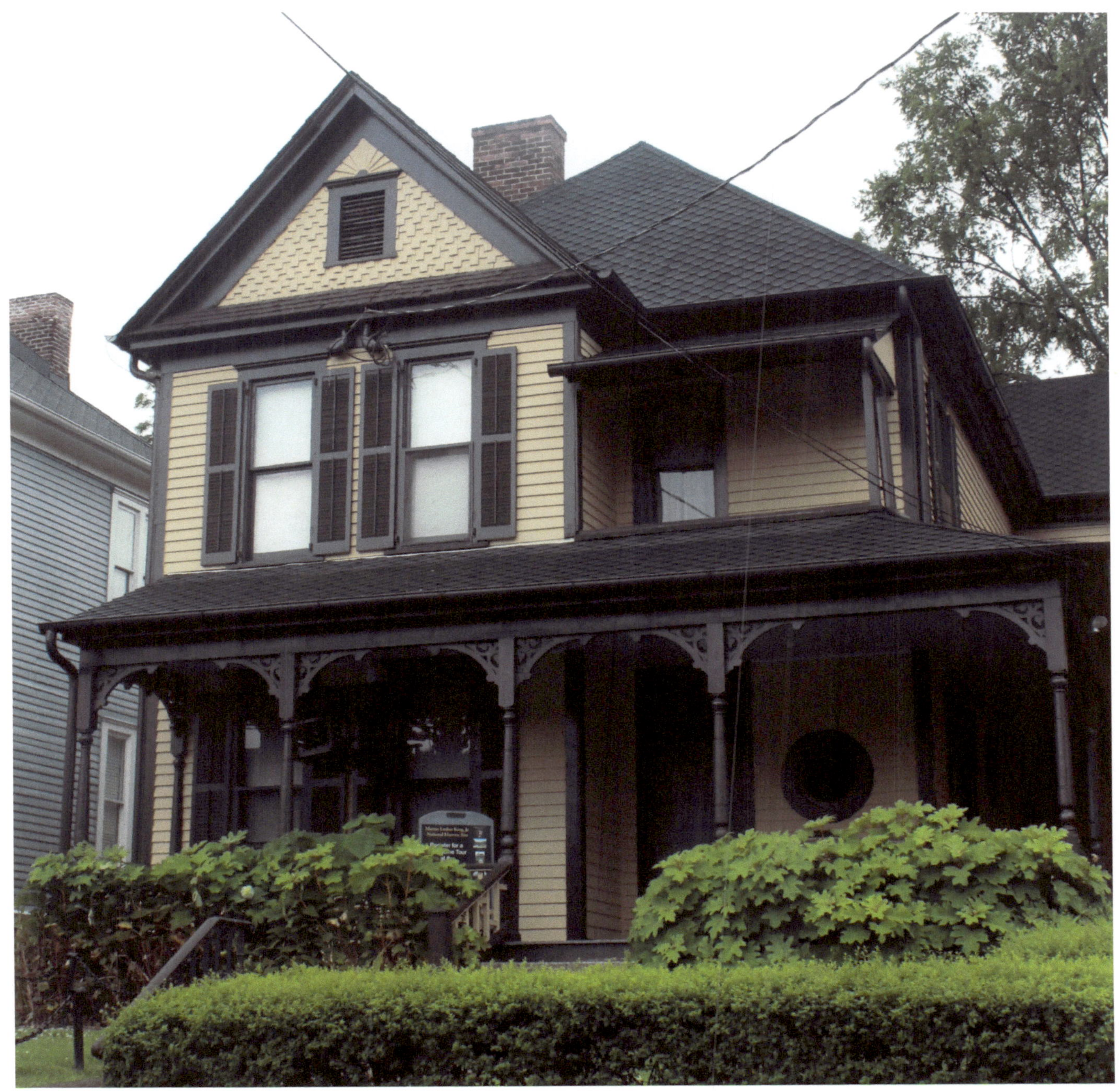

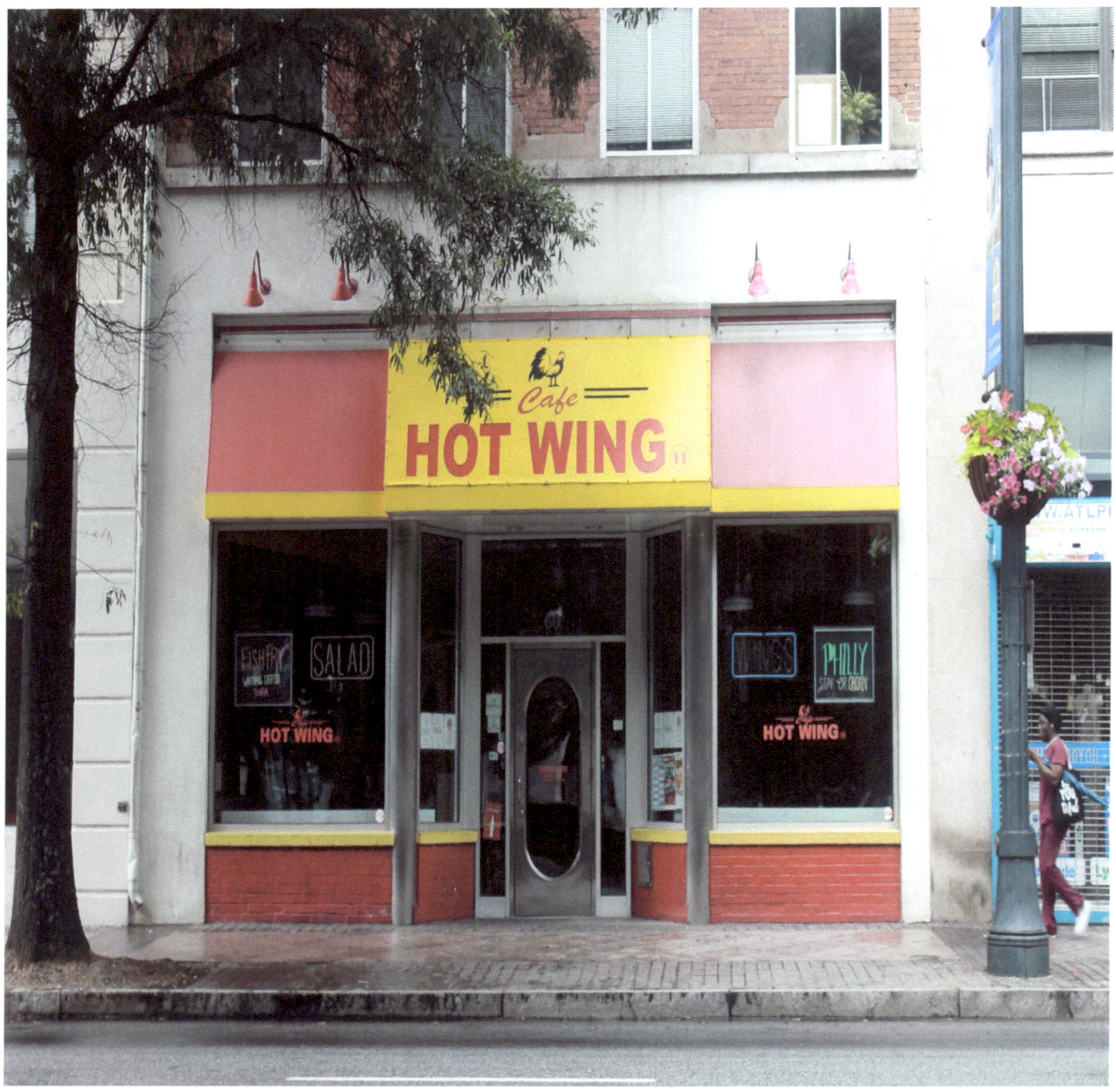

Cafe
HOT WING
FISH FRY
SALAD
HOT WING
PHILLY
HOT WING

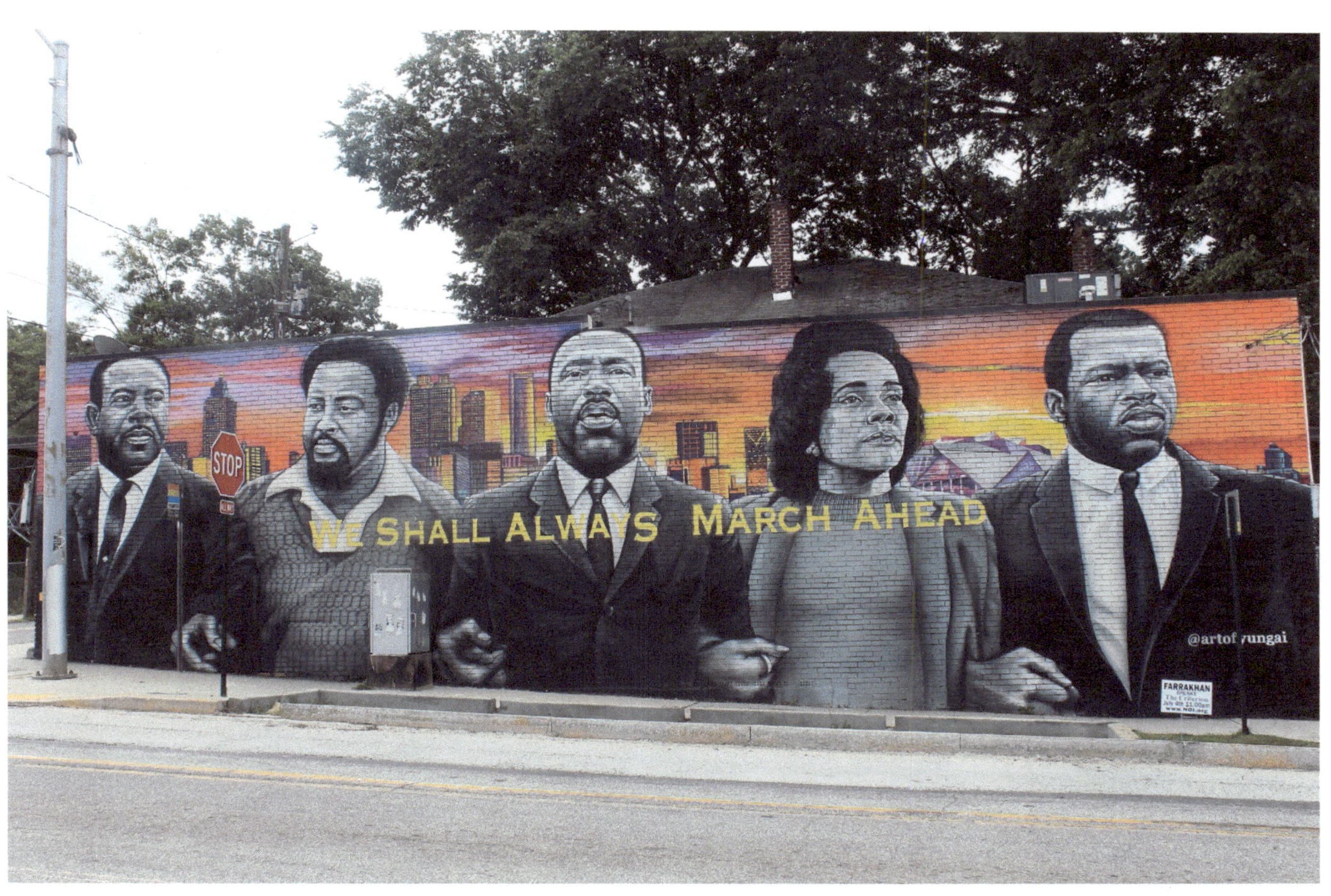
STOP
WE SHALL ALWAYS MARCH AHEAD
FARRAKHAN
www.NOI.org

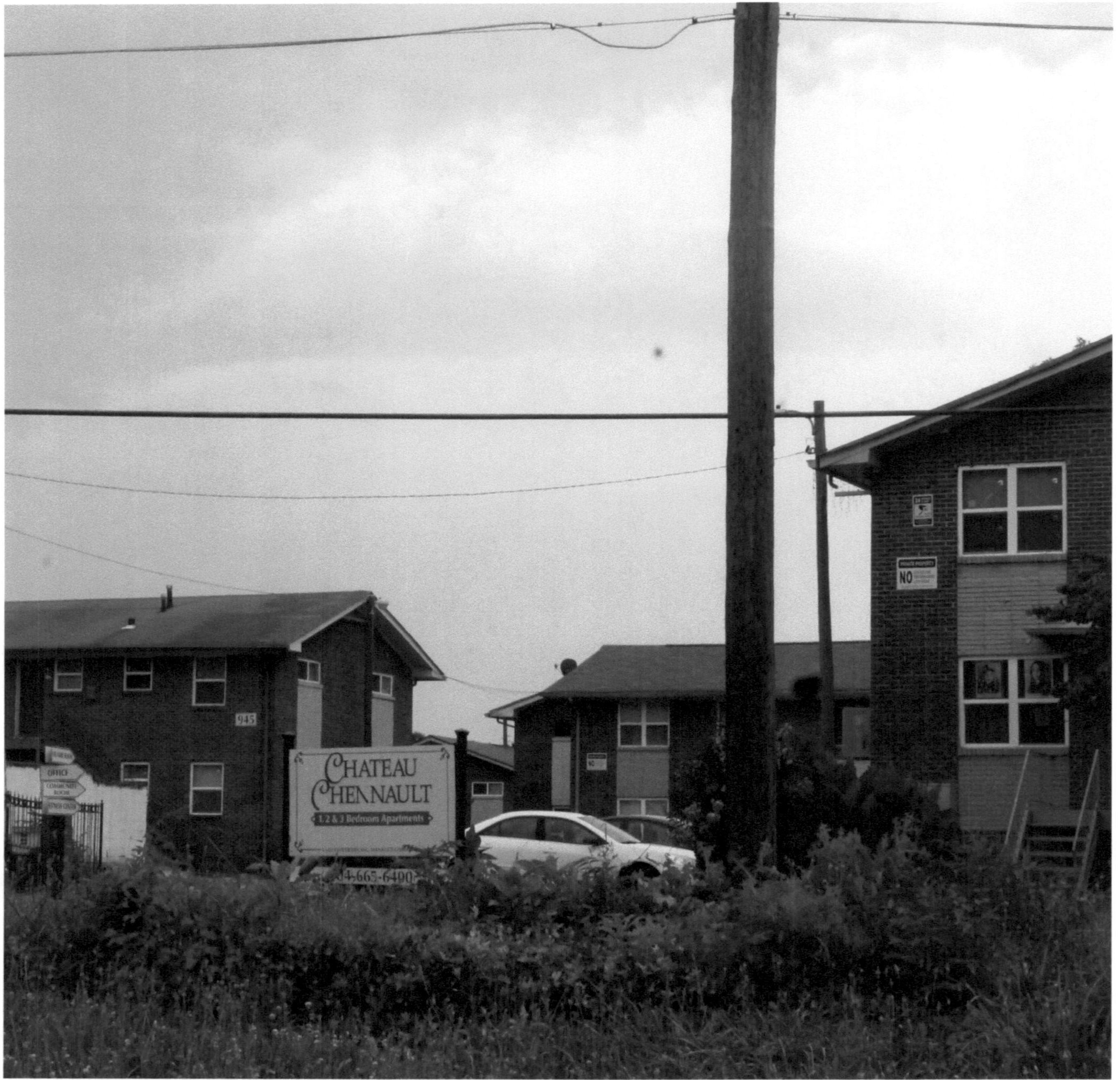
945
OFFICE
CHATEAU
CHENNAULT
1, 2 & 3 Bedroom Apartments
NO

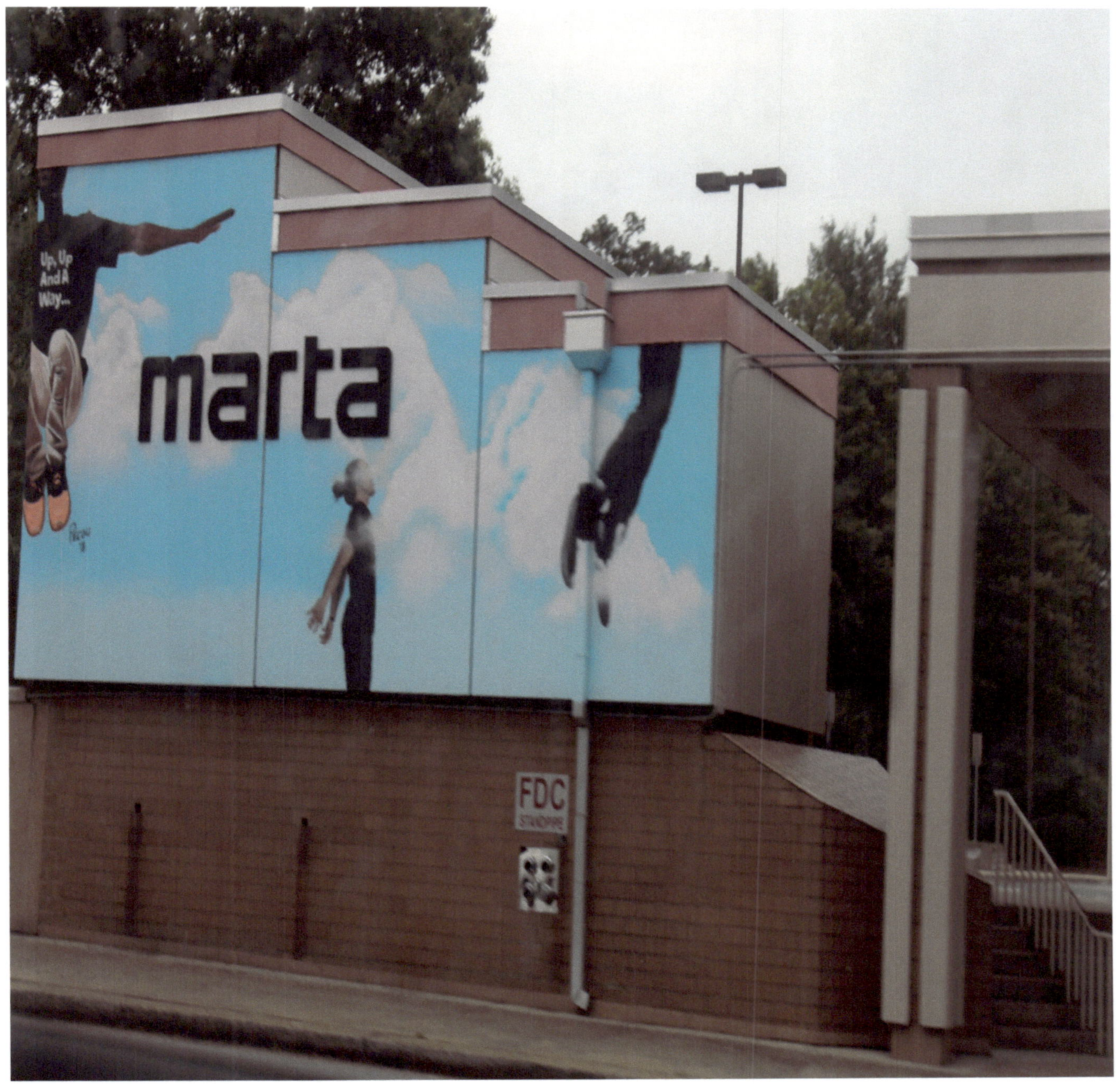
Up, Up
And A
Way...
marta
FDC

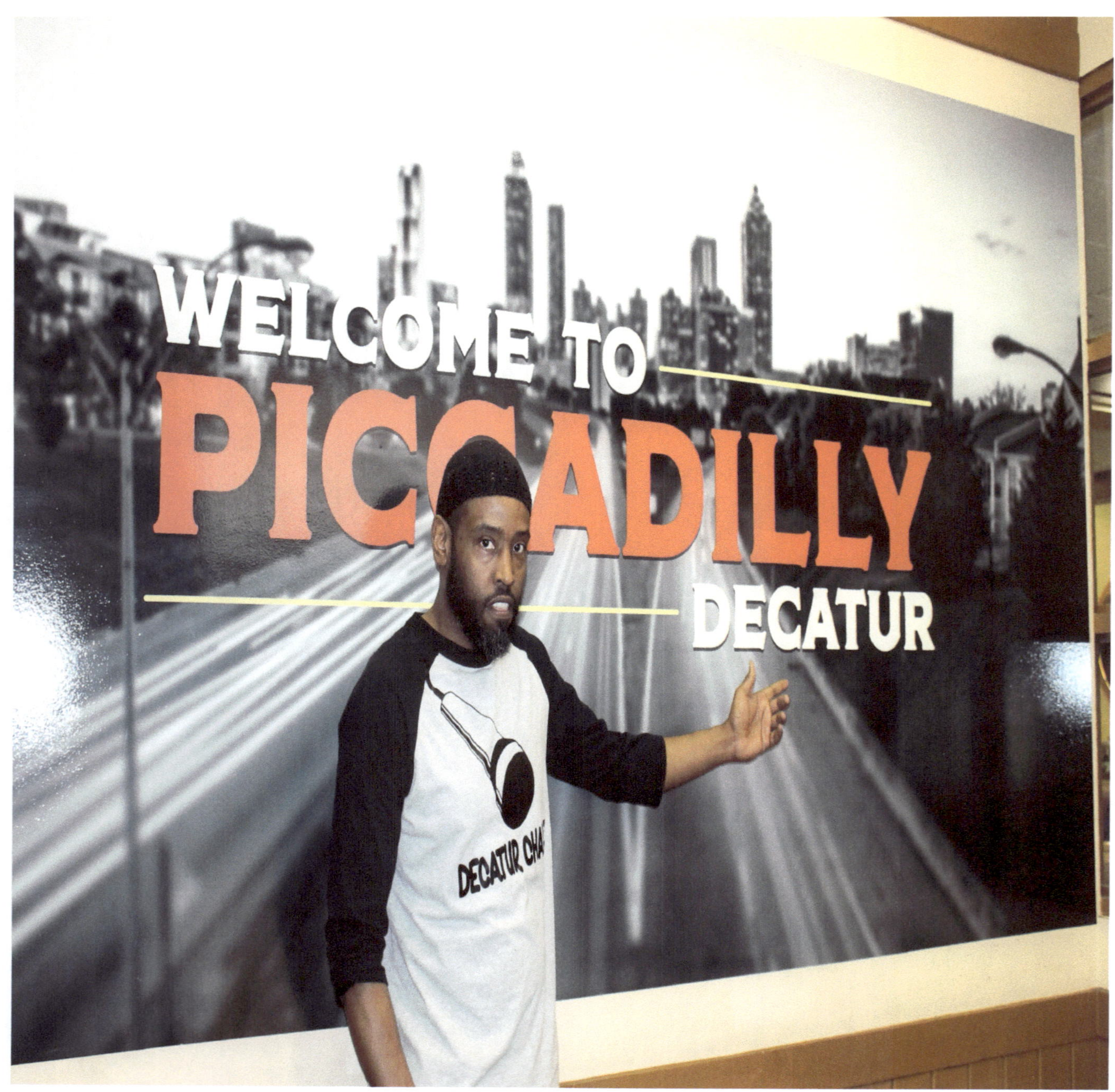
WELCOME TO
PICCADILLY
DECATUR

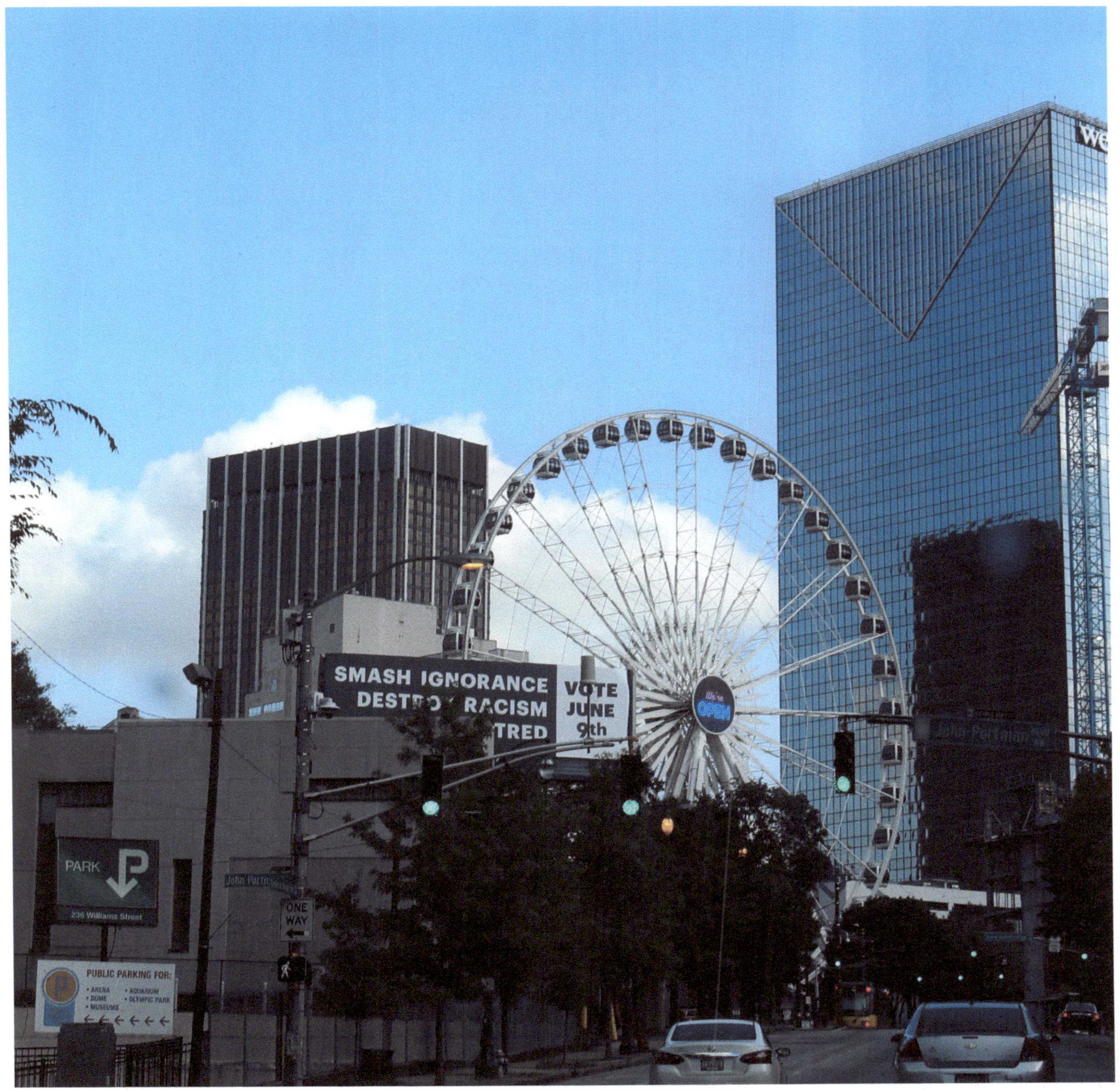
SMASH IGNORANCE
RACISM
VOTE
JUNE
9th
PARK
230 Williams Street
ONE WAY
PUBLIC PARKING FOR:
• ARENA • AQUARIUM
• DOME • OLYMPIC PARK
• MUSEUMS

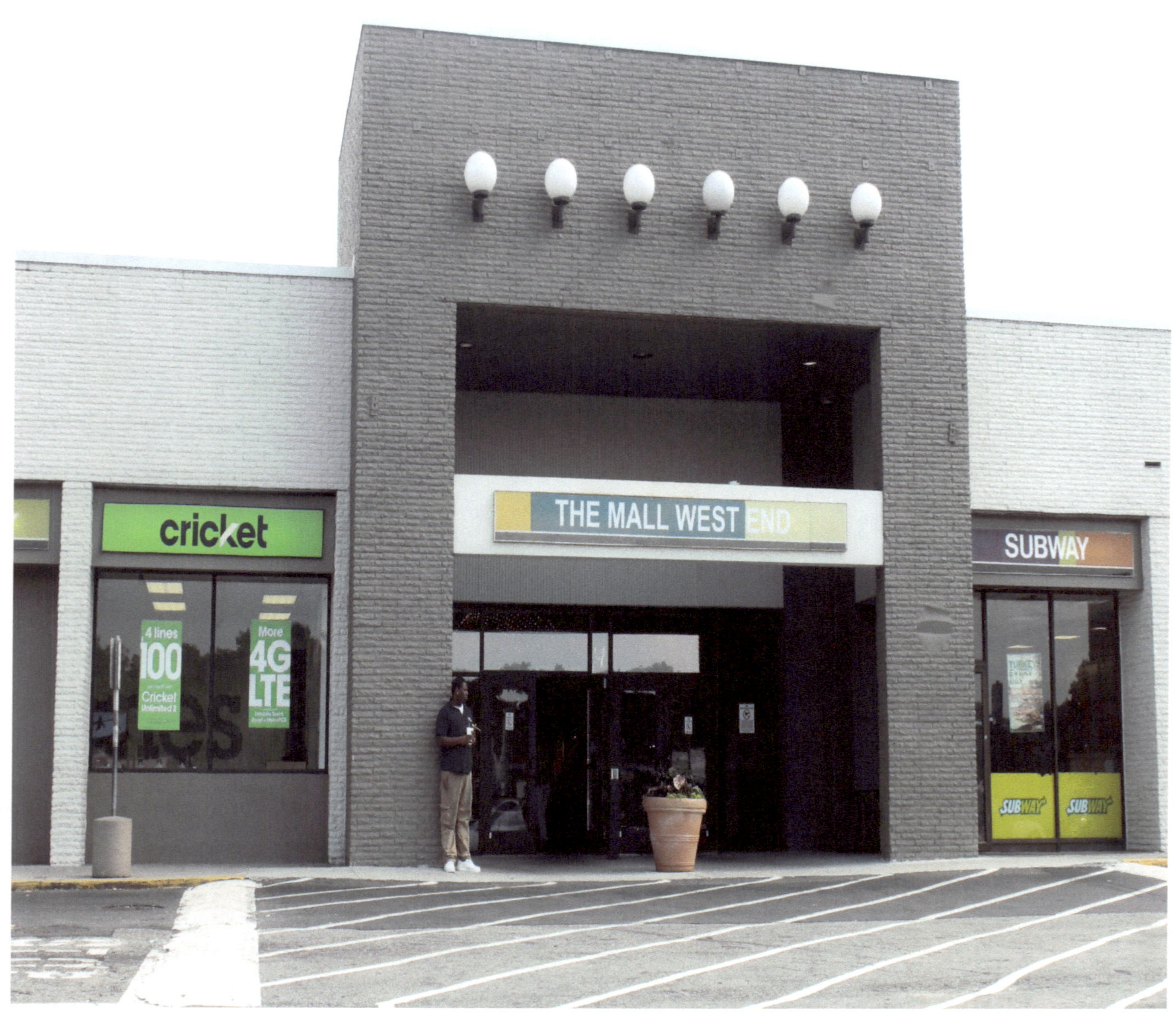
cricket
THE MALL WEST END
SUBWAY
4 lines
100
Cricket
Unlimited 2
More
4G
LTE

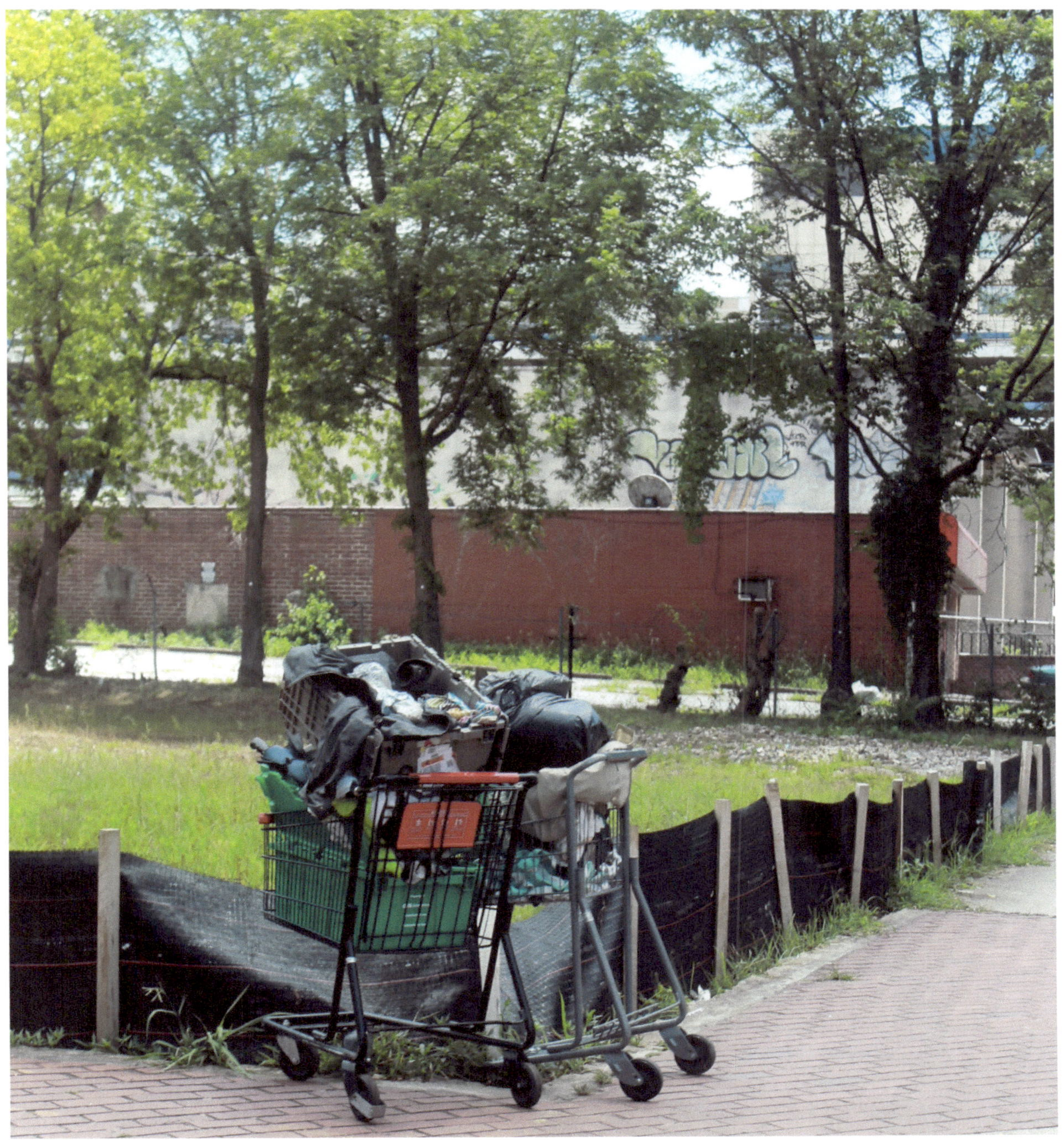

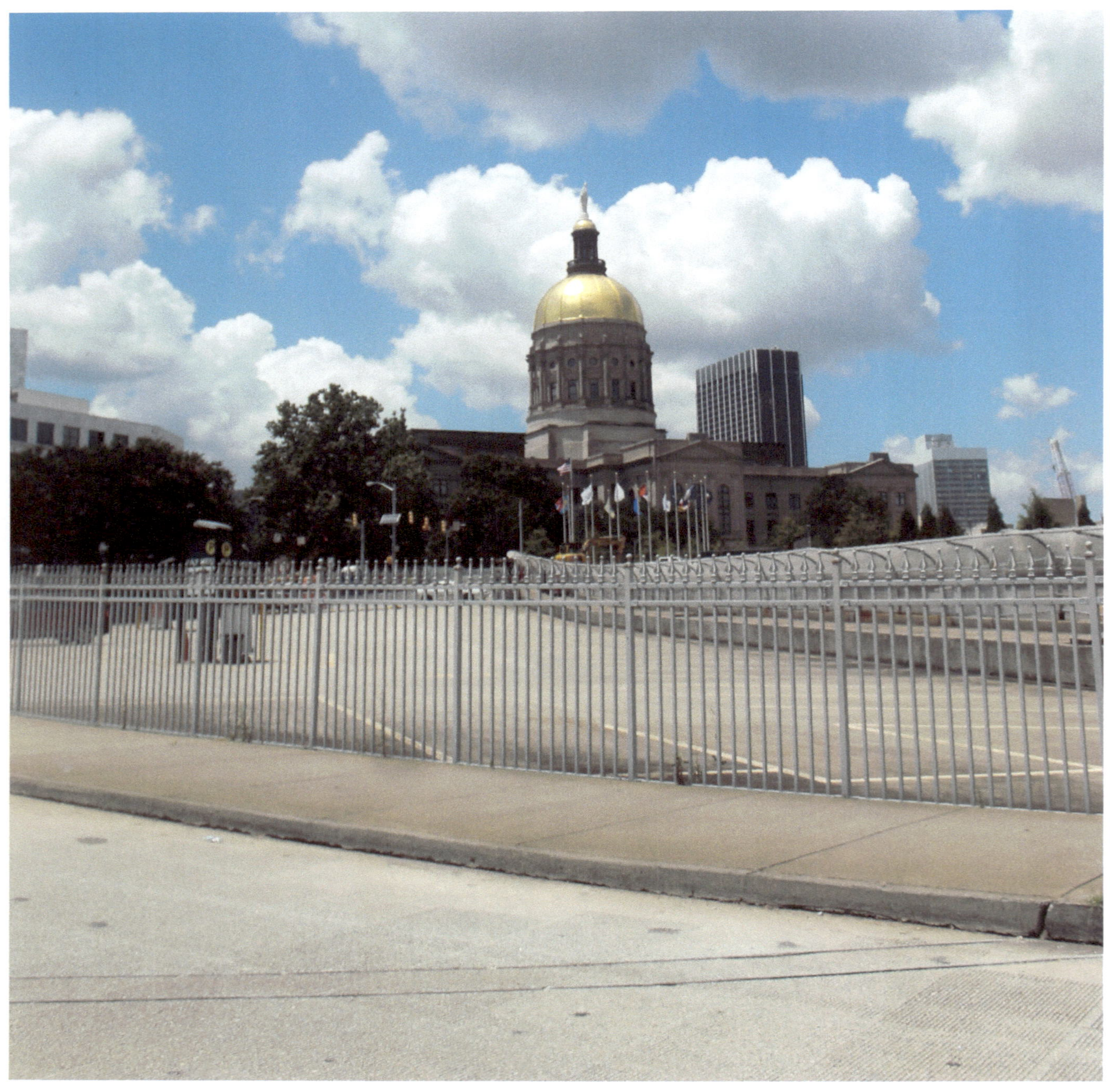

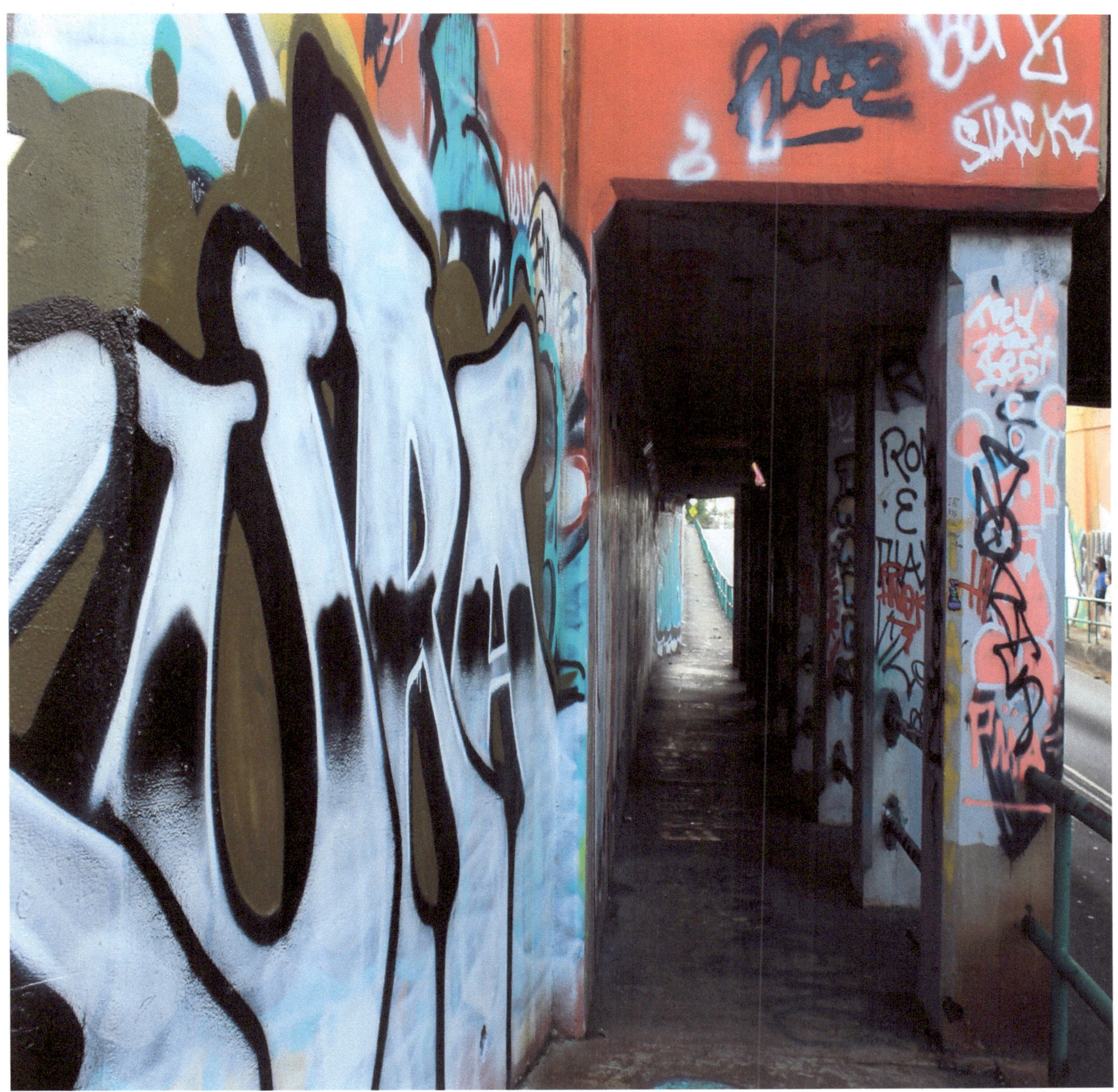

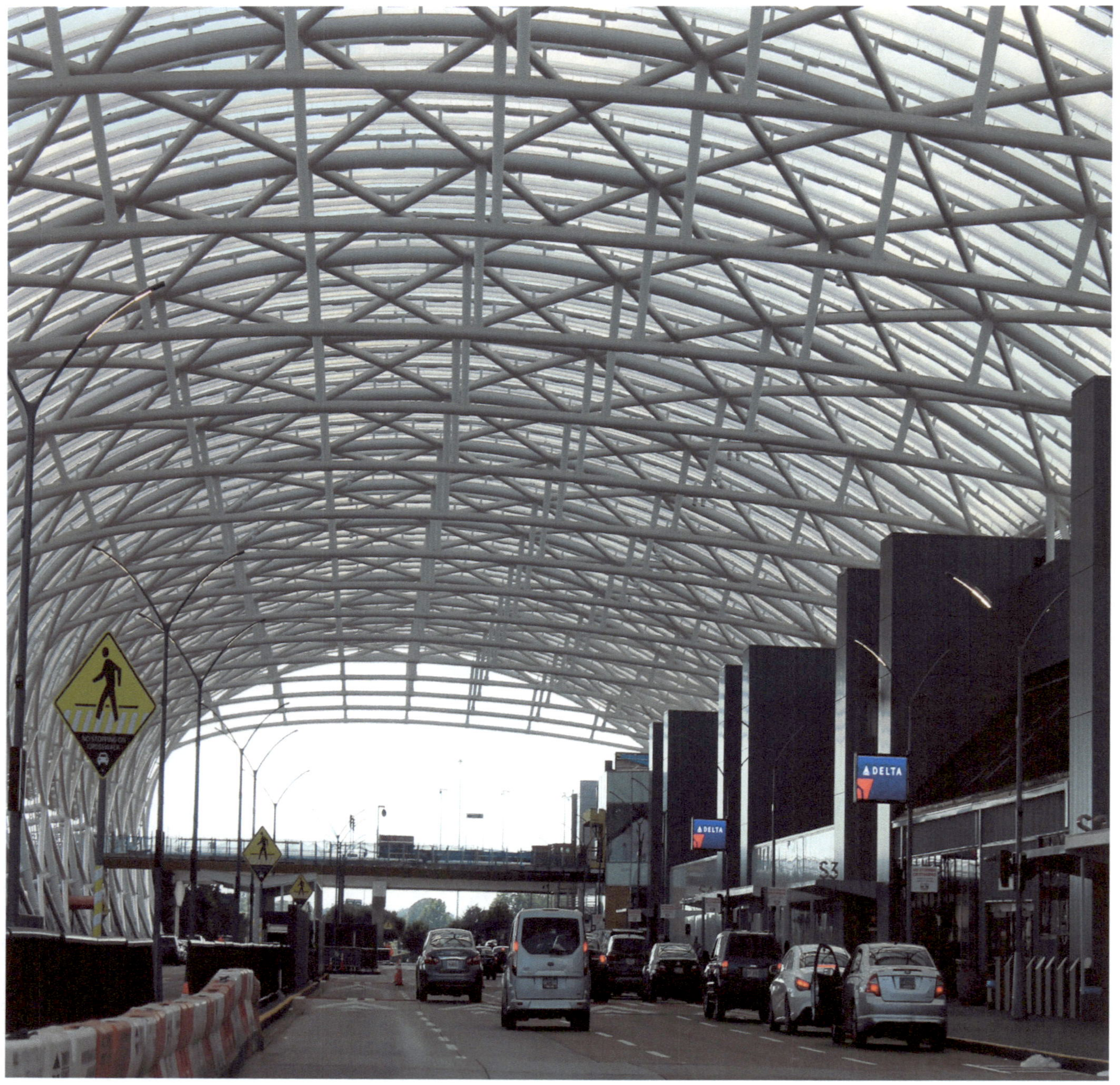
DELTA
DELTA
S3

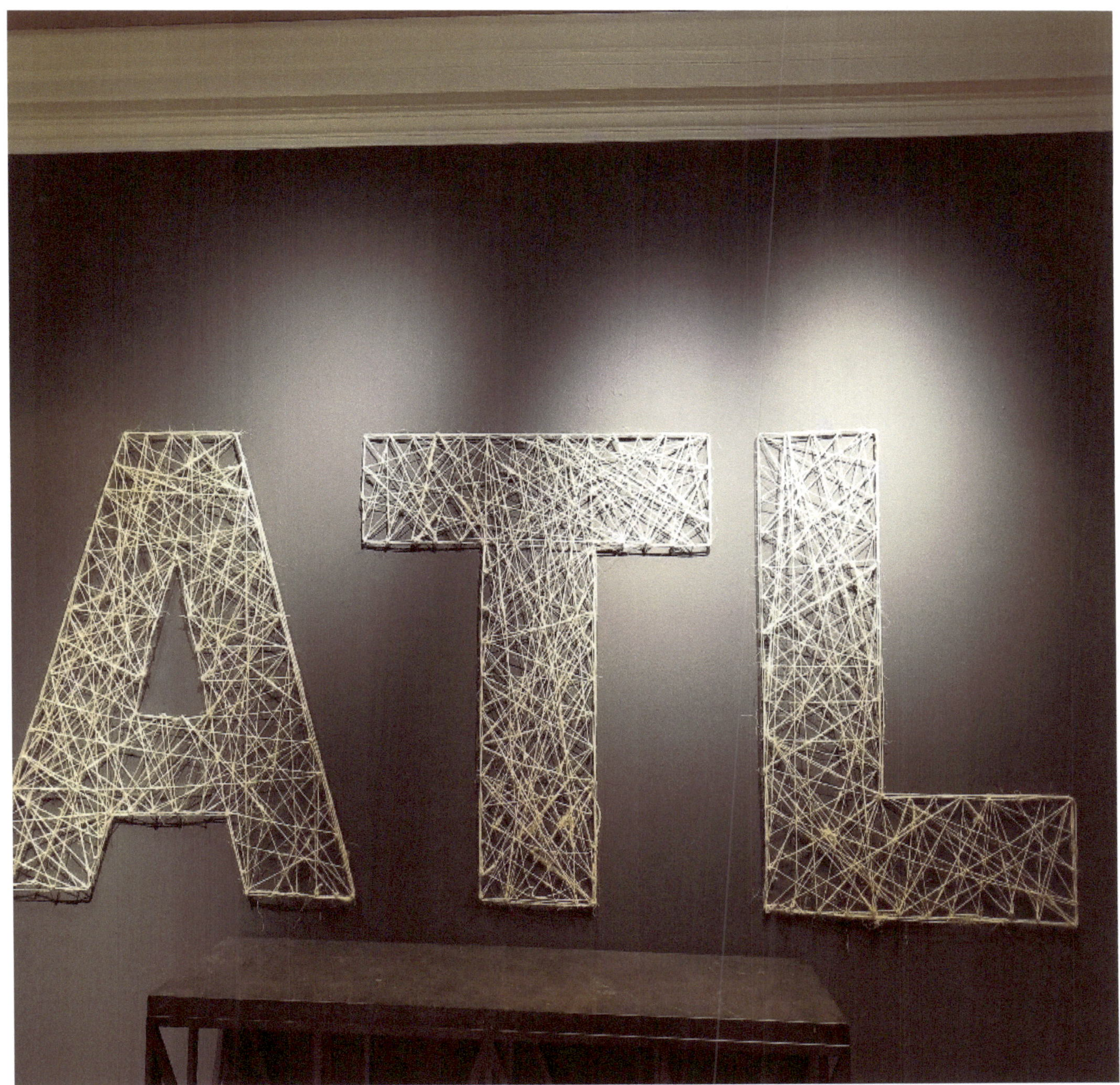
ATL

stand up

first u must have the motivation to stand
with a hand
in the air
to show that you care
stand up

yeah i know people may stop
and may stare
but who cares
go head and teach em bout the courage to dare
stand up

go head and help em feel the pain that you bear
stand up

go head and let them see the tears that you wear
stand up

then they can understand the struggle we share
stand up

stand up for something
show the people you're proud
be creative
and stand out of the crowd
stand up

speak your peace and make sure that you are loud
until they hear your voice and start to allow
stand up

their minds to wonder why and figure out how
or else your only choice will be to stand down
face down

with your ass on the ground
and a gun
to your back
cause you Black
and you're proud
so stand up
stand up

get up
get out
let's shout
stand up

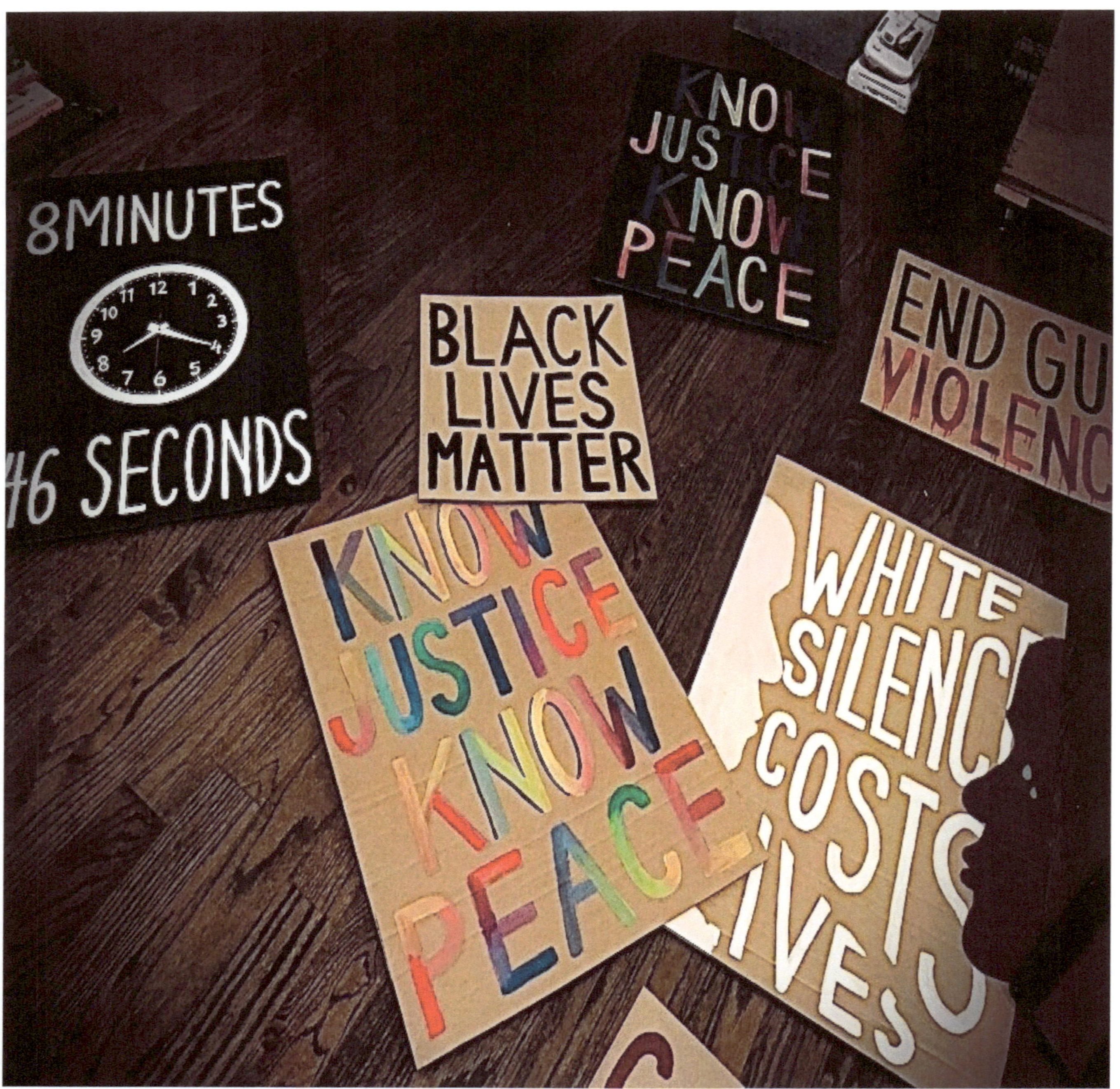
8MINUTES
46 SECONDS
KNOW
JUSTICE
KNOW
PEACE
BLACK
LIVES
MATTER
END GU
VIOLENC
KNOW
JUSTICE
KNOW
PEACE
WHITE
SILENC
COSTS
IVES

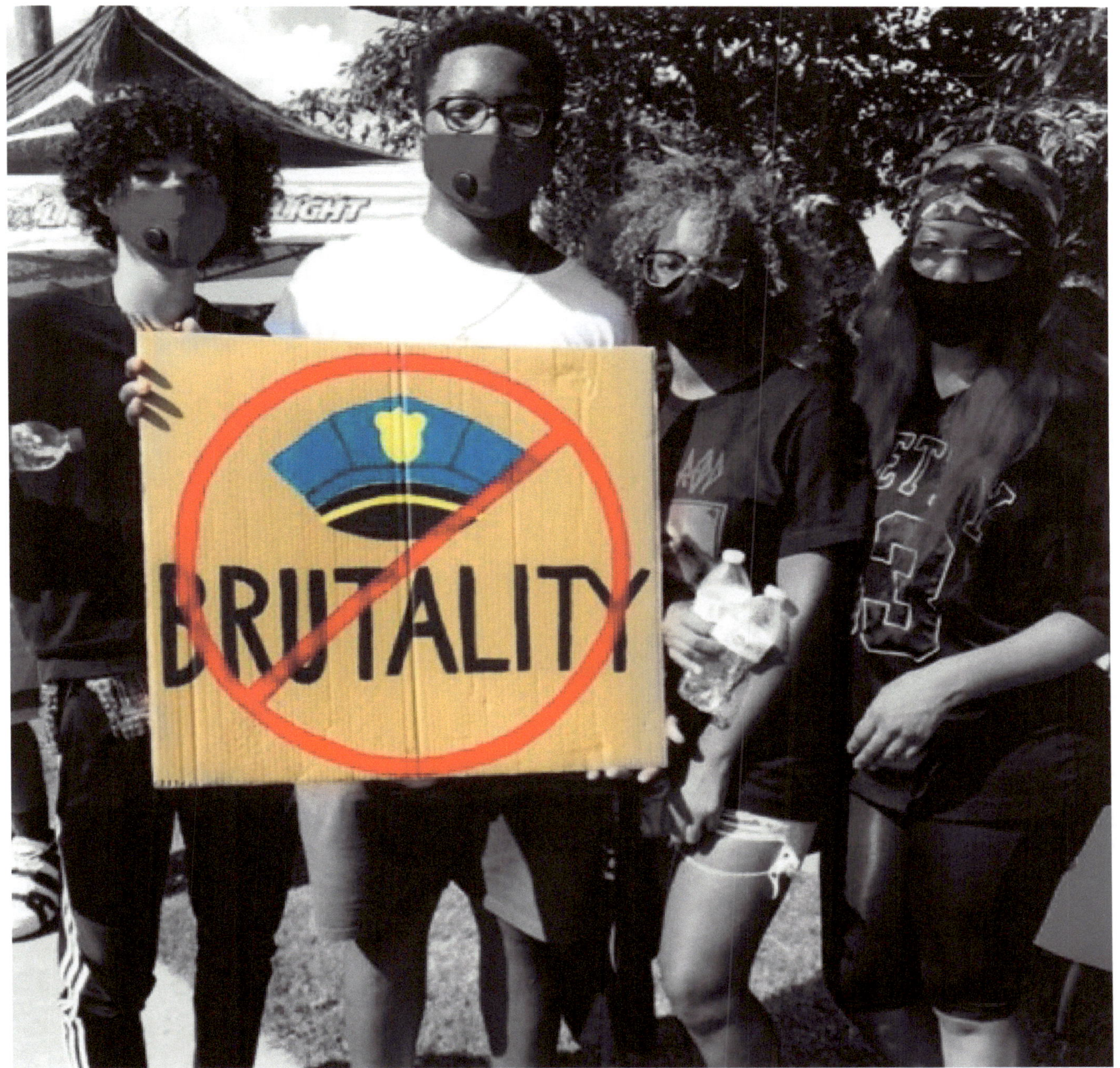
BRUTALITY

dizzy

i had went up
then i went down
then i went round and round and round
till in my ears there was no sound

blurry visions in my head
i aint hear what u had said
can u say that just one mo time
the world is spinning in my mind

i lost my balance and fell down
and when my body hit the ground
i felt like i'd been dranking Crown
high off life and liquor brown

i had went east
and i went west
and where i went
i wore my best
thought you would too
but then i saw
that dress you wore
not cute on you

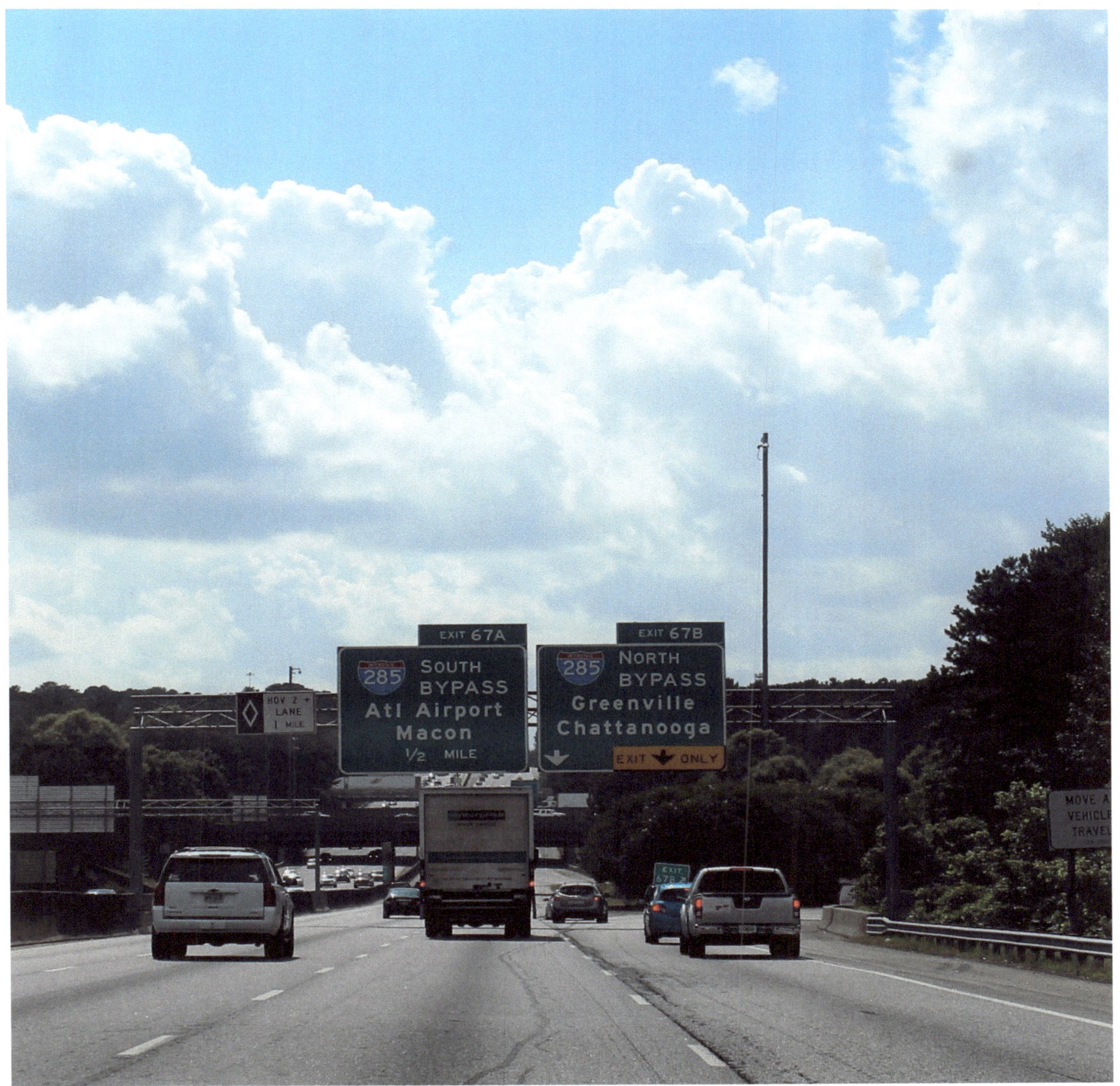
EXIT 67A
285 SOUTH BYPASS
Atl Airport
Macon
1/2 MILE
EXIT 67B
285 NORTH BYPASS
Greenville
Chattanooga
EXIT ONLY
HOV 2 + LANE 1 MILE

Blessings

Each day the sun breaks through the clouds
And rays of light
come shining down
Blessings shower over me
Like drops of rain
they fall so free
Unannounced
beyond my dreams
Sometimes I think “All this for me?”
What did I do to deserve this love?
These random gifts
from up above
Somebody must have prayed for me
God blessed my soul so I could see
His love and grace
abundantly

Another day has come to be

The sun breaks through the clouds again

And blessings still

come down like rain

On me and all of those who I love

Like rain they fall from up above

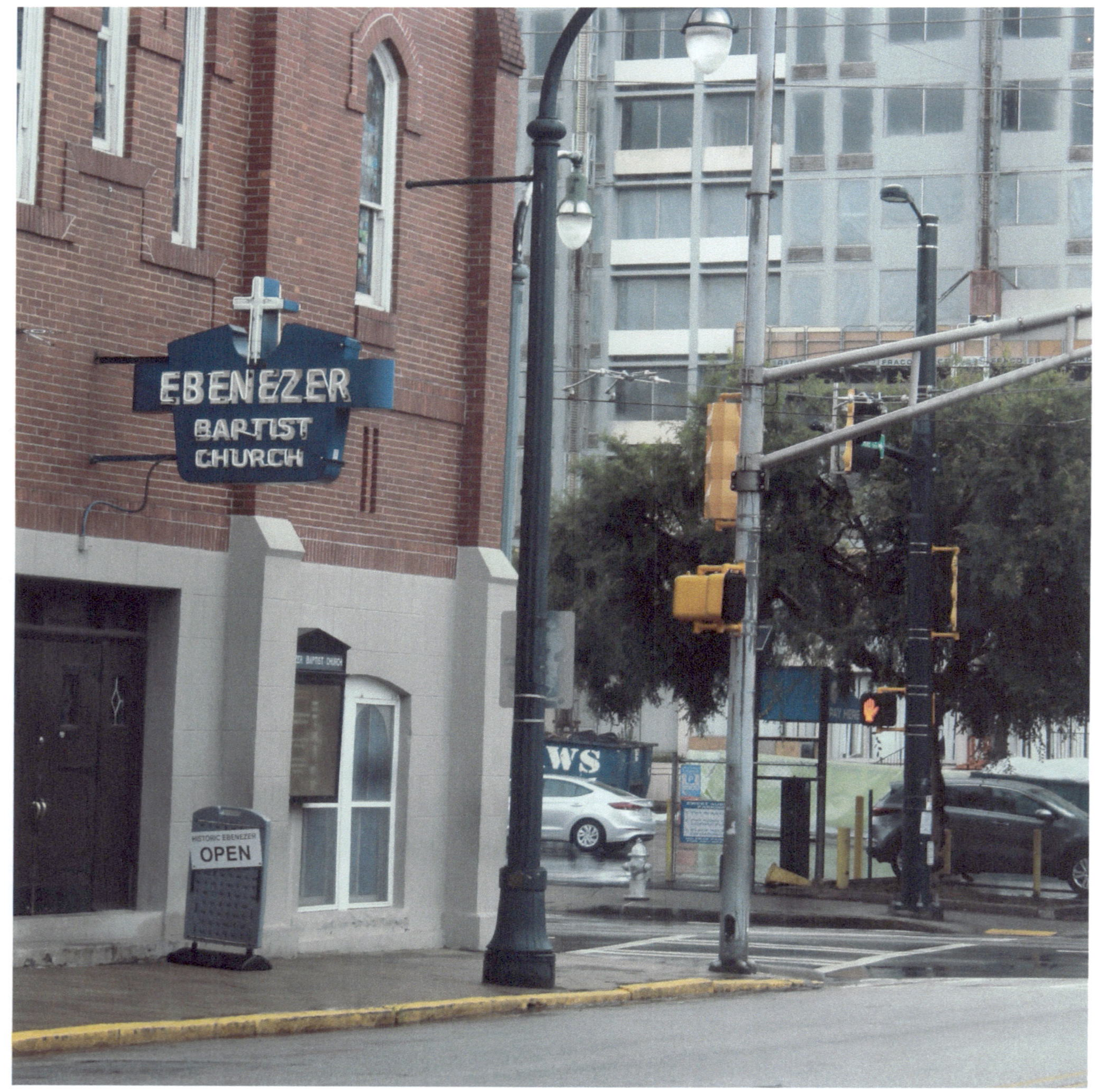
EBENEZER
BAPTIST
CHURCH
HISTORIC EBENEZER
OPEN

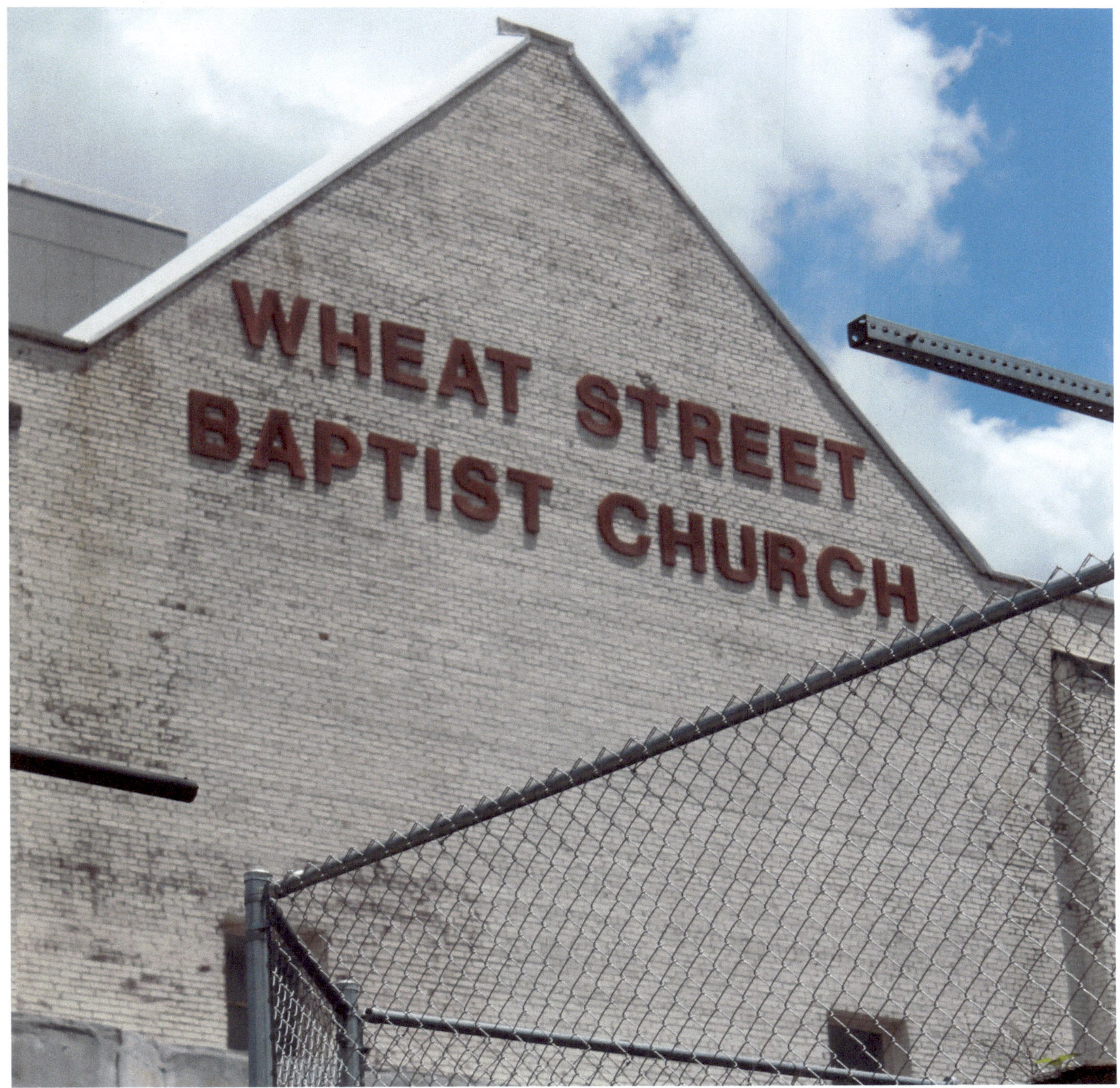
WHEAT STREET
BAPTIST CHURCH

The Come Up and The Hate

Haters reach out so they can cop a feel
They so jealous, can't believe it's really real
They stand back with their hands on their hips
Pouting hard with heavy bottom lips
They suck their teeth and they roll their eyes
They just mad because you won the prize
Don't sweat it cause the come up is real
Just keep rising like Maya said, "And Still"
Keep cheesing cuz the hate will never stop
It won't stop you from getting to the top
The Come Up
The Hate
So what's the debate?
Don't wait til too late
To create
your
fate

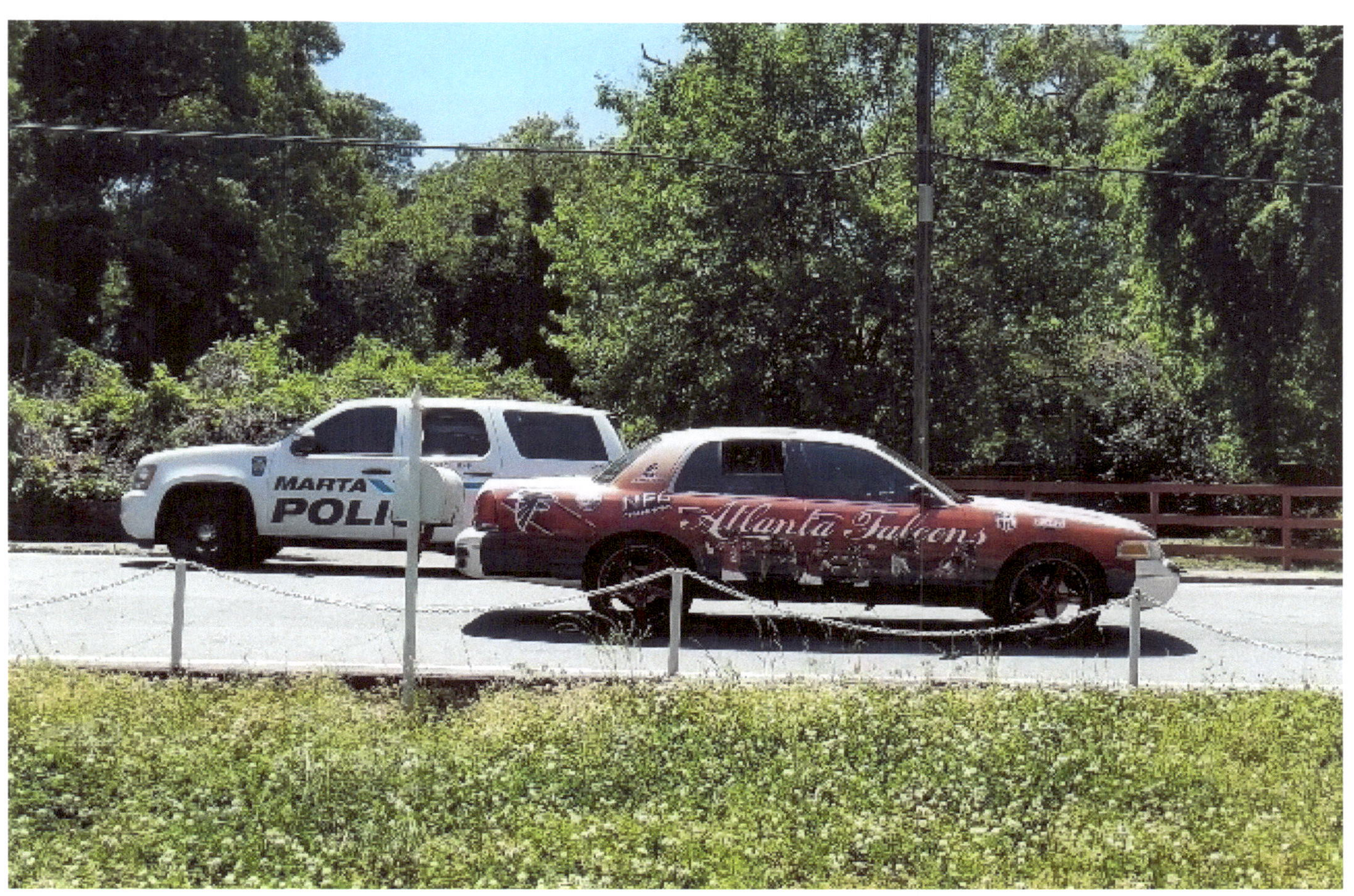
MARTA
POLI
Atlanta Falcons

The Metro

Atlanta is not just a city it is a metropolis
Some cities you may not have even heard of but they are synonymous
To the ATL where we reside
from the north to the south to the upper east side
Cobb on 75 North and Gwinnett on I-85
It's gon take you 4 hours to get home if you get caught there after five
The Southside has Fayette, Henry, and Clayton too
East Point College Park is Atlanta through and through
Back in the day most Black folks stayed inside 285
Aint no more housing projects now it's all gentrified
To the East there is Stone Mountain, Lithonia, and Decatur
Home to many athletes and rap stars, yeah it's greater
Douglasville is to the west, out past Six Flags Park
It's still a little rural so be careful after dark
Atlanta is not just a city it is a metropolis
Maybe one day its residents can live harmonious

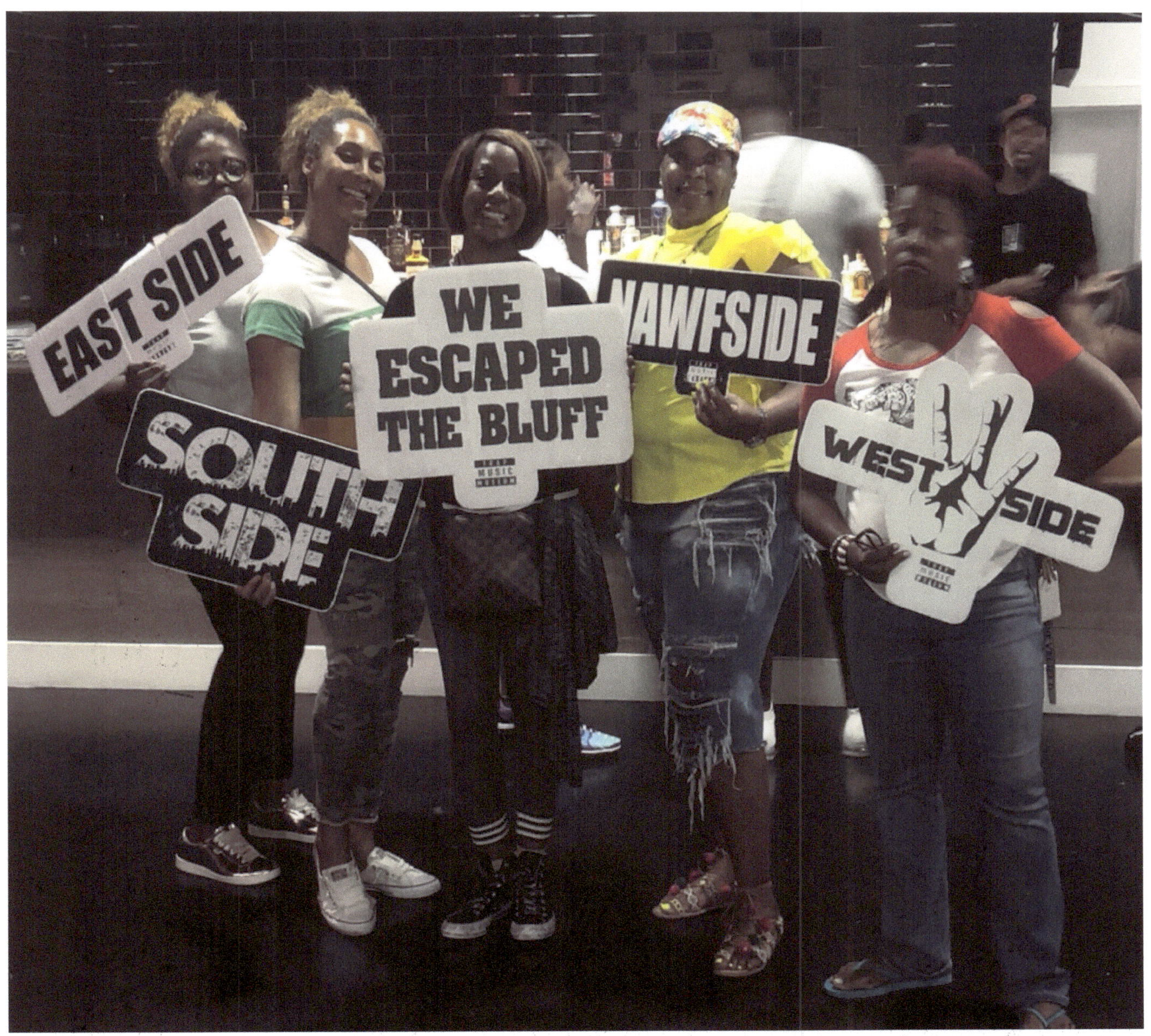
EAST SIDE
SOUTH SIDE
WE ESCAPED THE BLUFF
NAWFSIDE
WEST SIDE

We Moving On

We moving on, we on the roll

Got a mission to accomplish and a bounce up in our stroll

We got somewhere

we have got to be !!!!!

Places to travel,

and folks to see

We moving on up

we're on the go

We're moving forward

to our goal

Some tracks are fast

other trails are slow

Some journey's take time with room to grow

Pathways may twist

and turn and bend

Before we're ready

sometime they end

Wherever you going stay on the move

It's time to segue to another groove

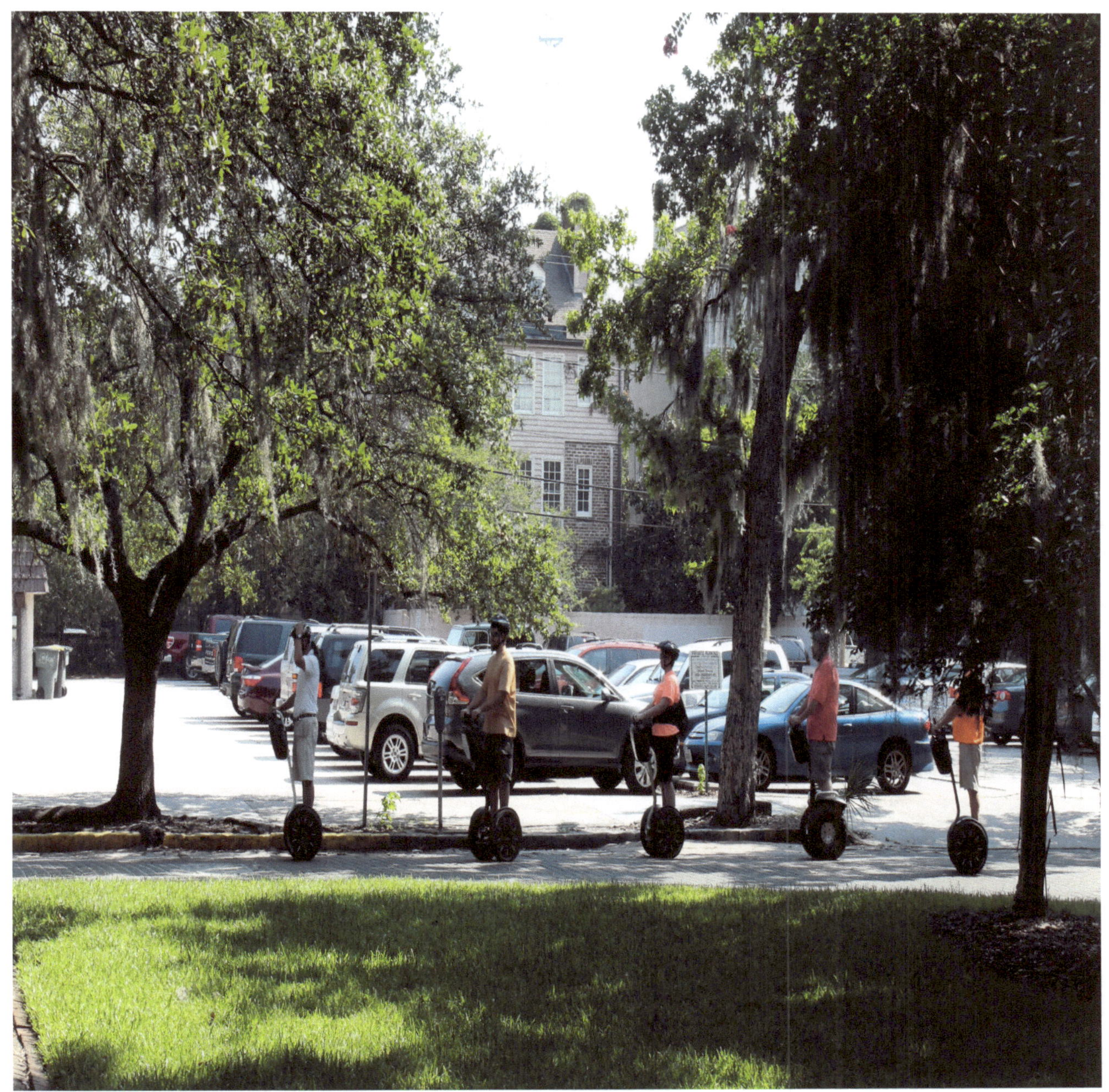

Untitled

The ocean that washes the sand

The sounds of my favorite band

Your sun kissed skin so tanned

My breast cupped in your hand

Just a few of my favorite things

If you knew me you'd understand

Walking on a moonlit beach

The exquisite taste of the perfect peach

Listening to my pastor preach

Appreciation for my freedom of speech

Just a few of the things I love

All my goals are within my reach

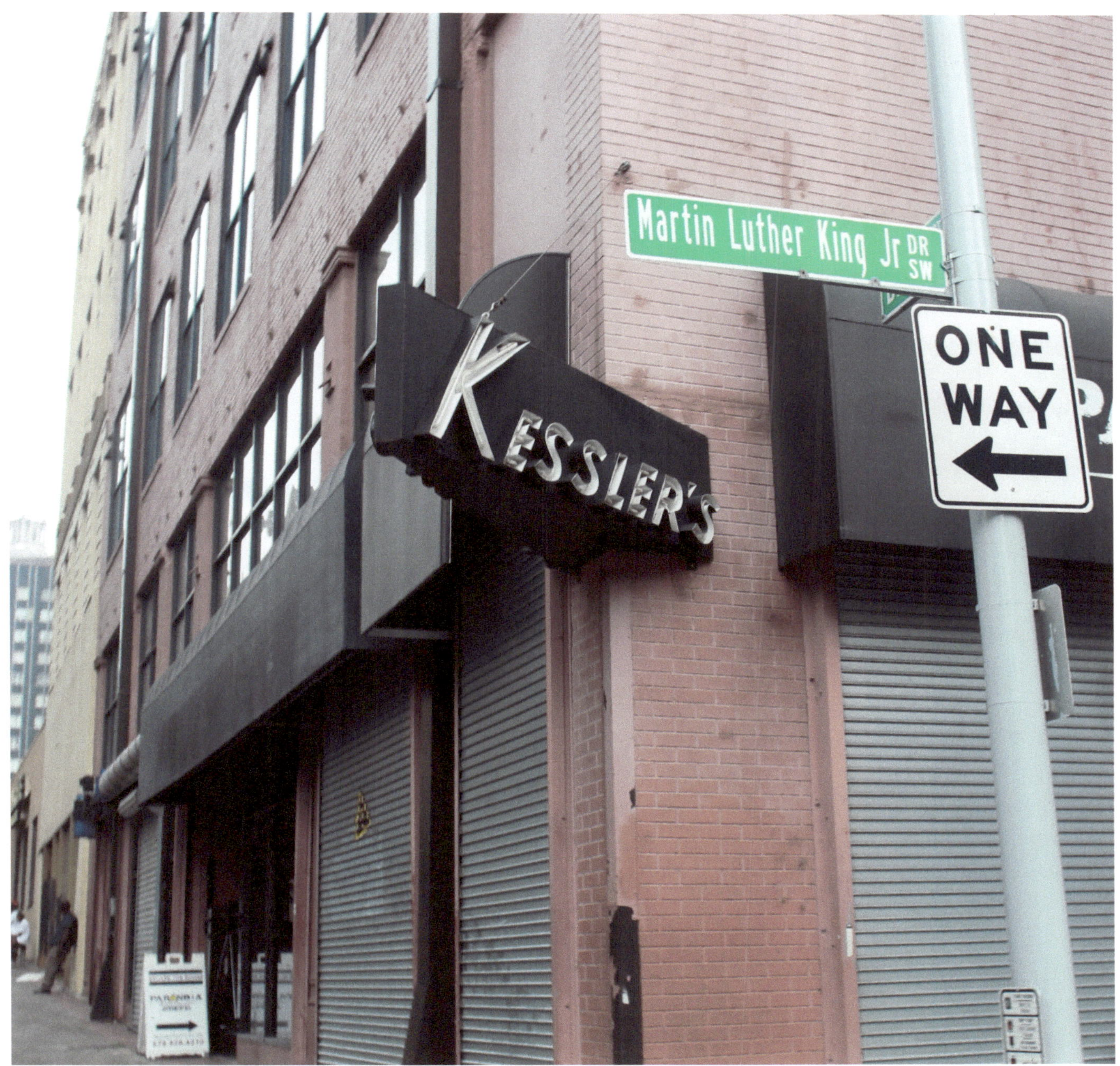
Martin Luther King Jr DR SW
KESSLER'S
ONE WAY

poetlife

apparently you ain't got to rhyme
all the time
to be a poet
you can just write about
whatever's on your mind
random thoughts
you know it
throw words together
that sound good together
weave and sew it
discuss birds in flight
and the moon and stars at night
just flow it
and compare love to water
and sadness with trees
like
winding rivers and dogs with fleas
use your
list of SAT words
so with lots of luck
all who read your sh$% won't be wondering
what the fuq?

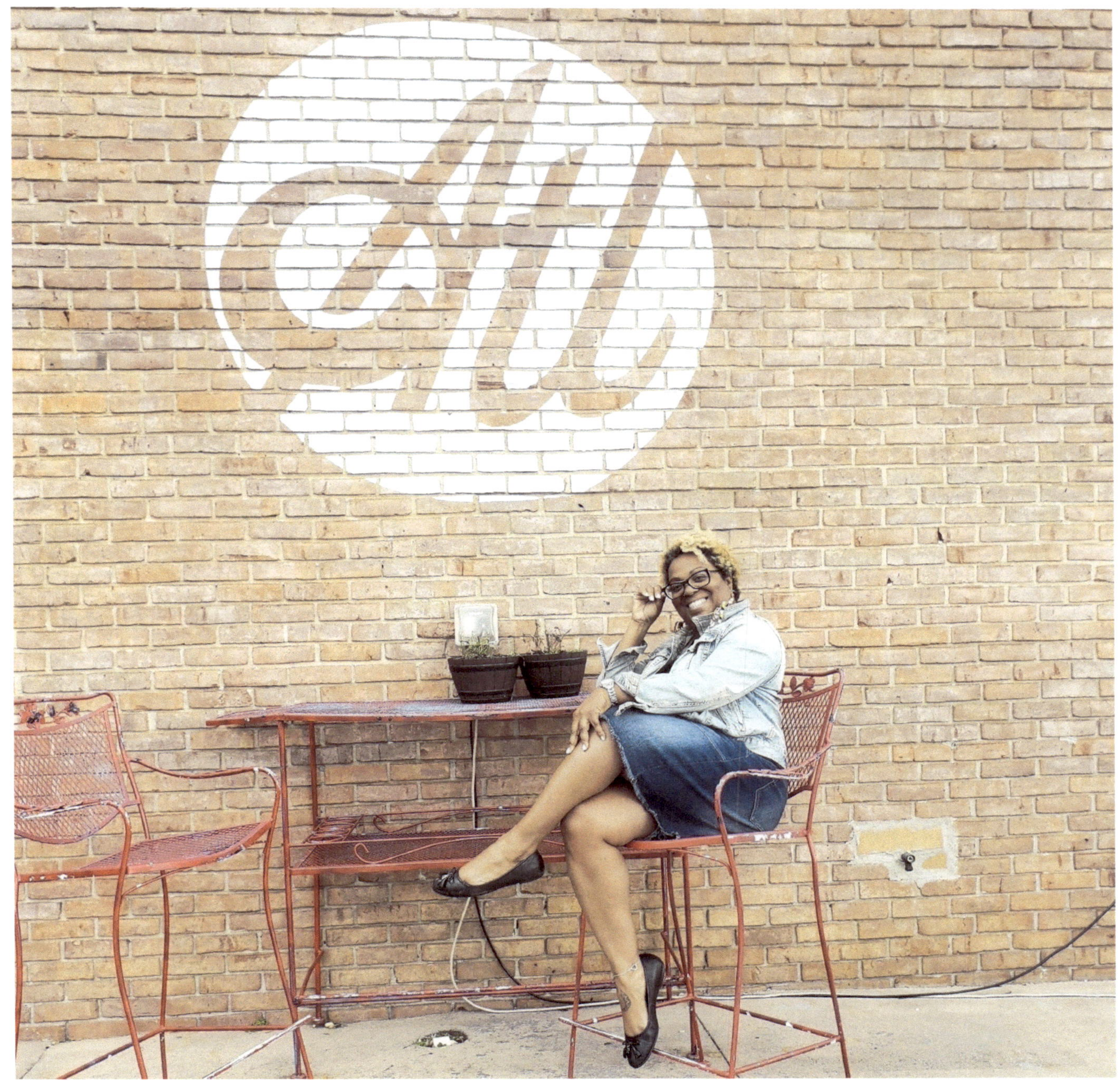

Faith

With open arms I leap off of the ledge
and fall into the wide abyss
of the unknown
descending upon my destiny
hoping and praying along the way
my wildest dreams and ideas
will come true
before I land
before I rest
before I'm ashes
dust to dust

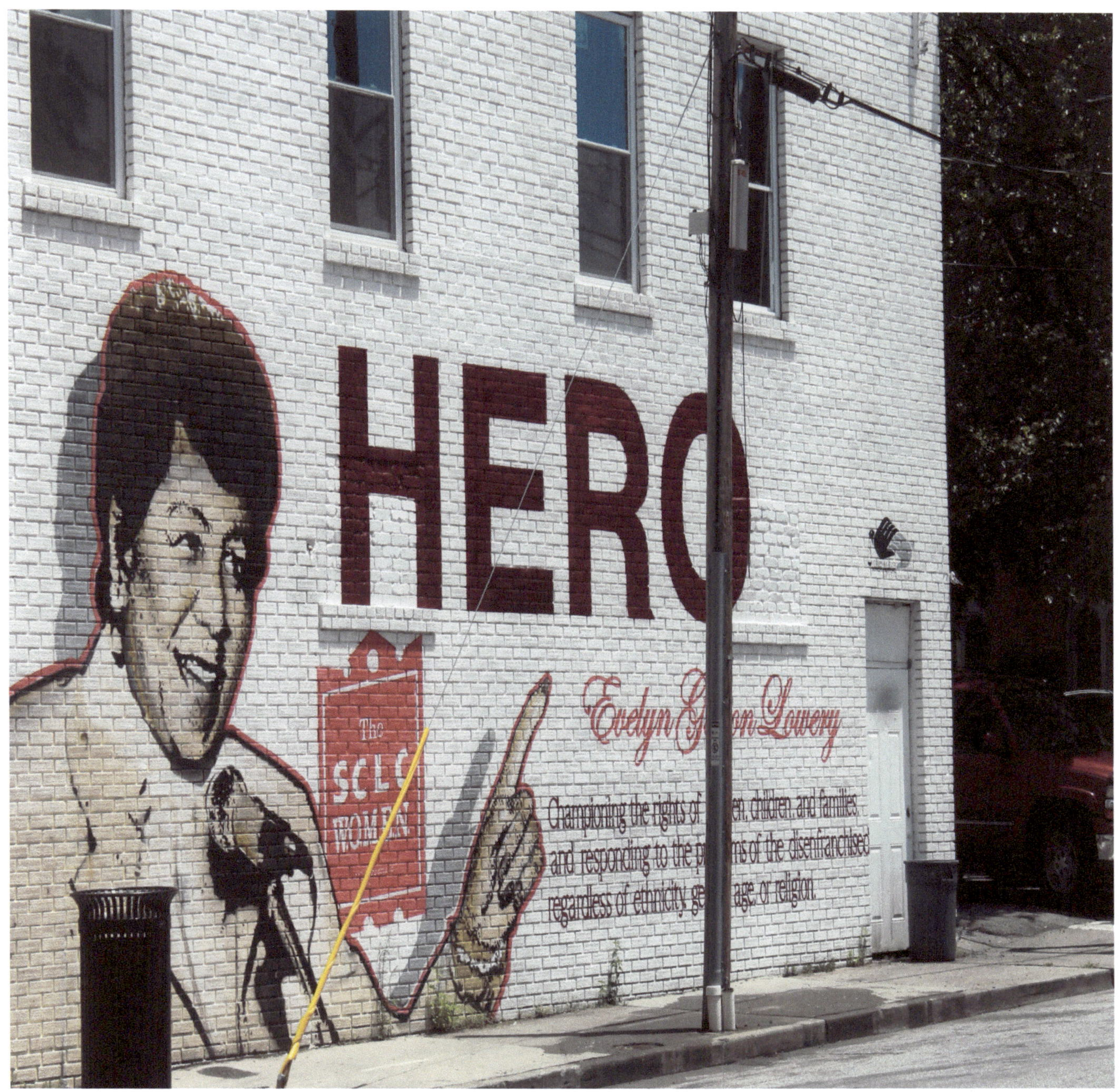
HERO
The
SCLC
Lowery
Championing the rights of
children, and families,
and responding to the
of the disenfranchised
regardless of ethnicity,
age, or religion.

A Love Letter to Outkast

Dear Big Boi and Andre (Hey Ya!),

What can I say, it seems like only yesterday, when I heard y'all first hit, man and it was the sh&t. I was a junior at UGA, had just pledged in 94, and we needed a song for our step show. We needed something crunk, yet slow. I asked, "You heard about them two boys from the A? They got a single out that I heard on the radio the other day."
It goes, "all the players came from far and wide" the step master listened to it and that's the song we played, when we went on stage. I've been in love ever since with the beats, they "so fresh and so clean". I'm in love with the lyrics, with the performances, and videos. I'm a true fan of your work that you put in at the studio. You motivate us to "get up, get out, and get something" and taught us all that "music makes the world go round".

I knew ya'll had crossed over when that double album dropped, *The Love Below* and the *Speakerboxx*. Man that was genius, two experiences in one. And I just knew when I saw *Idlewild* that y'all would get an Oscar for the cinematography alone or at least the soundtrack and songs, would get a Grammy or two, for "Moving Cool".

I remember standing up at Centennial Olympic Park, in the dark, waiting on the concert to start. My mind going crazy wondering what would be the first ballad sung. I was like its got to be "B.O.B". and sure enough I heard "1, 2, 1, 2, 3!" And I screamed and closed my eyes and in my mind I was in Bowen Homes jumping in convertible cars and running on purple lawns.

Big Boi I saw you at a concert at the College Football Hall of Fame, I was the girl in the front row screaming your name. Andre I met you in a clothing store at Little Five Points with my friend. When we walked in, you smiled and she asked could we take a picture with you and you pointed to a sign that said, "No photos Allowed" so I just bowed, and said, "All Hail to the Outkast".

Love
A Fran in the Stand

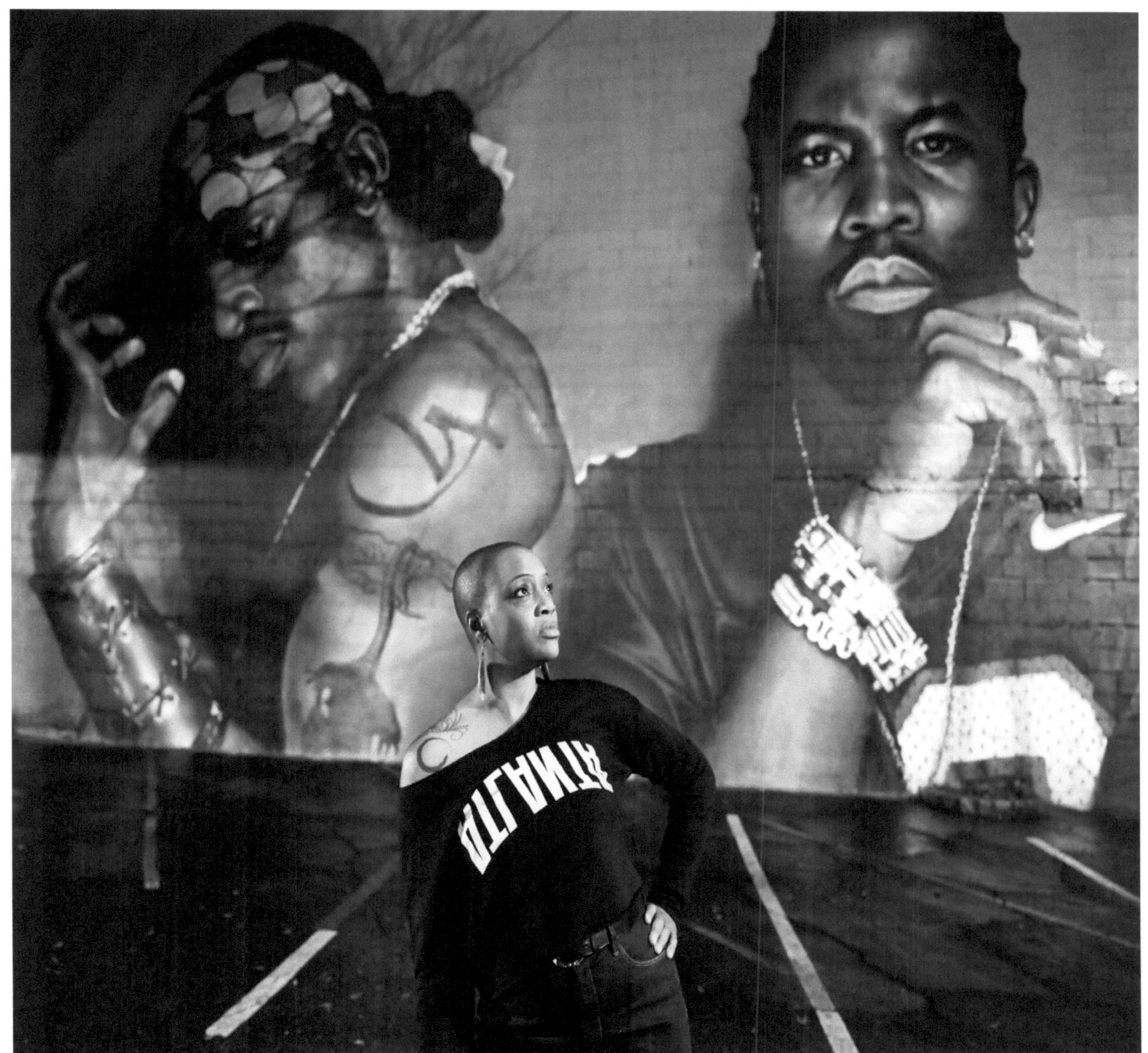

Freaknik

It was the biggest party, in the ATL for years
“Don’t stop get it get it “ was all that I could hear
How did a small get together of college kids and Greeks
Morph into utter chaos, a picnic full of freaks?
“Round and round we go” was on the radio
as they closed all of the exits and shut down all the shows
All the clubs were packed out. So what did we do?
We start dancing on the hoods of cars and freakin random dudes
It was a lot of booty popping, a lot of smoking weed
A lot of club hoppin, and dranking liquor in the street
“Gimme a bottle and a big ol cup!”
“Shake what ya mama gave ya!!!” “Wsup wsup?!”
The police could not contain the crowds. It was so many here.
People came from far and wide to shake their derriere.
I went in 1994 and again in 95.
It was the crunkest time I’ve had, in my entire life.

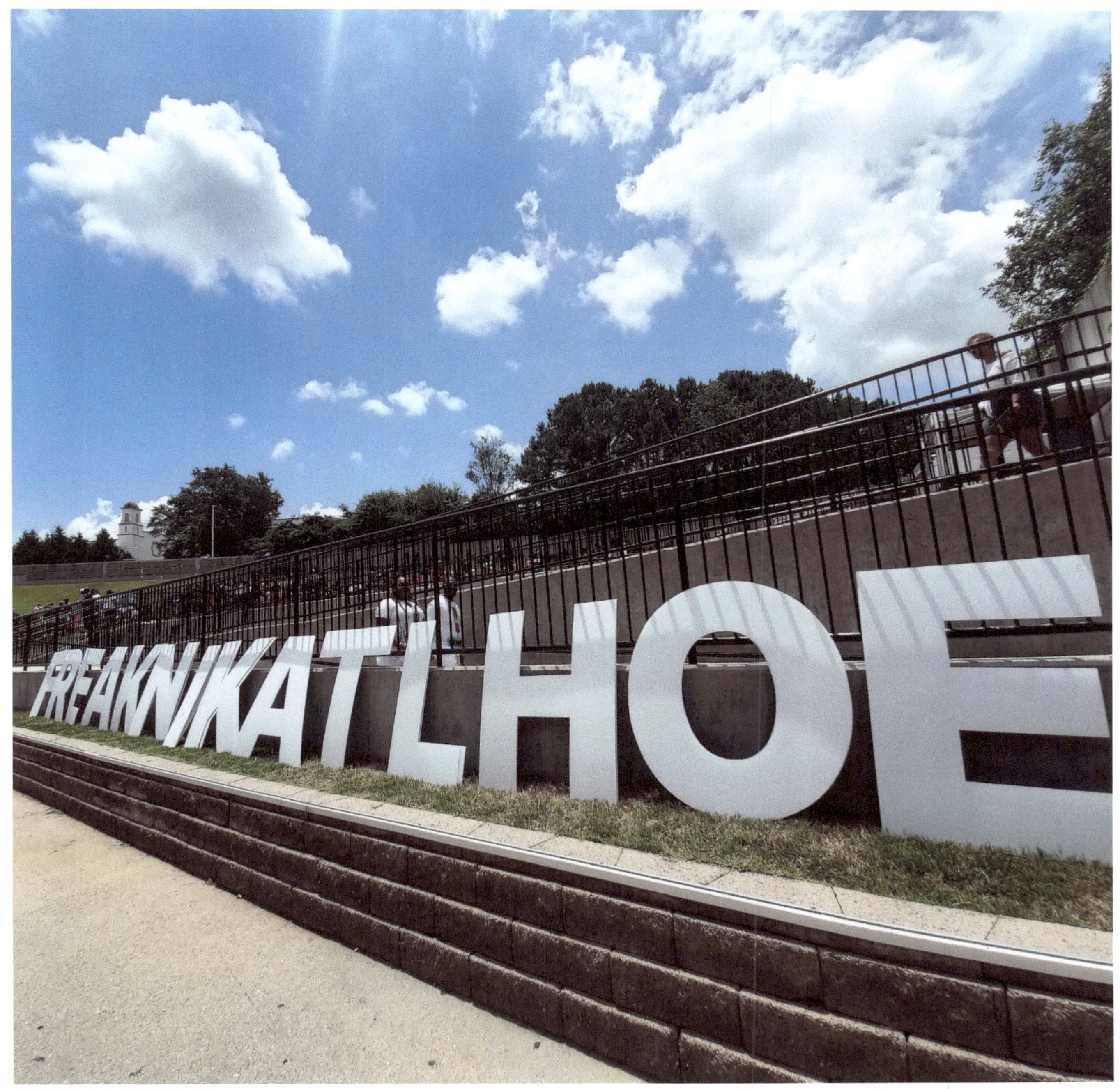
FREAKNIKATLHOE

The Fabulous Fox

My first time at The Fox
I dressed in church attire
Soft green velvet with creme lace socks
and large silk ribbons in my locs
Butterflies in my tummy fluttered as I left the bus
and walked upon the crimson carpet underneath a sky of lights
It was so beautiful
More extravagant than a cinema
and more people than the mall
We eased into our seats just as the lights began to dim
As the heavy curtain raised
The Alvin Ailey Dancers were on stage
Golden brown bodies swayed and long legs leapt
Arms sculpted, movements sharp
Synchronized yet graceful art
The sound surrounded me like a hurricane
and I was swept away in a whirlwind of culture
An experience I will always cherish
Our Broadway here at home

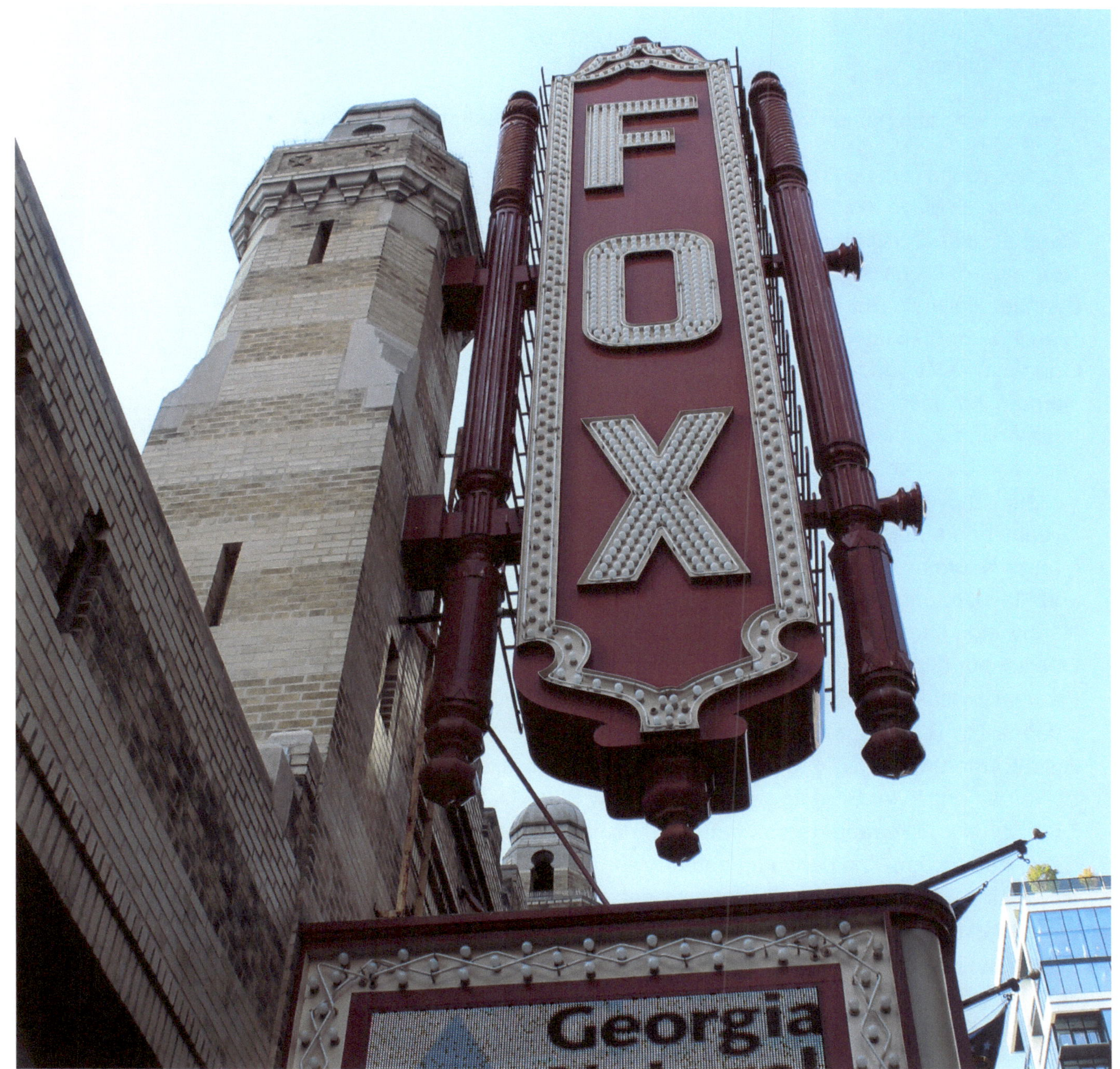
FOX
Georgia

Who is Atlanta?

There are certain names you say, that make you immediately think of the A

Andrew Young reminds me of the '96 Olympic Games
Benjamin E. Mays focused on education, wanted us to use our brains
Coretta Scott and Dr. King fought for civil rights and racial gains
Dominique Wilkins made me want to watch a Hawks Basketball Game
Evander Holyfield represented us with his boxing fame
Francene Breakfield hopes that one day all will recognize her name
Goodie Mob introduced you to the SWAT, the hood that I claim
Herman J. Russell built Atlanta, he changed our terrain
India Arie made us aware that having no hair should not be a shame
Jermaine Dupri and Jacquees welcomed you to Magic City and The Blue Flame
Keisha Lance Bottoms, our Boss Lady, is straight up running thangs
Lil John and Ludacris brought us crunk music. "OK!!!" we all now exclaim
Monica Kaufman brought us the news each night with her hair style always changed
and Maynard Jackson's leadership was so great he served twice, Airport renamed
Neon Deion had us doing The Dirty Bird at the Falcons games
Outkast put Atlanta on the map these kingz will forever ever reign
Pastor Troy said "We Ready" while the feds watchin 2 Chainz
Queens like TLC aint got time for no scrubs cause they too mundane
Ryan Cameron, our radio MC kept us laughing, he is insane
Spike Lee and Tyler Perry gave Atlanta its new Black Hollywood name
T.I. and Killer Mike rappers now activists encourage us to act humane
Usher had us throwing peace up and A town down as he entertained
Vick was our favorite quarterback I miss seeing him train
Willie Watkins you can trust to honor your loved ones last remains
Xcape just kickin it and asking for understanding as they sang
Ying Yang Twinz whispering, can't hear ,trying not to strain
Zat is the list from A-Z of some of our famous ATLiens

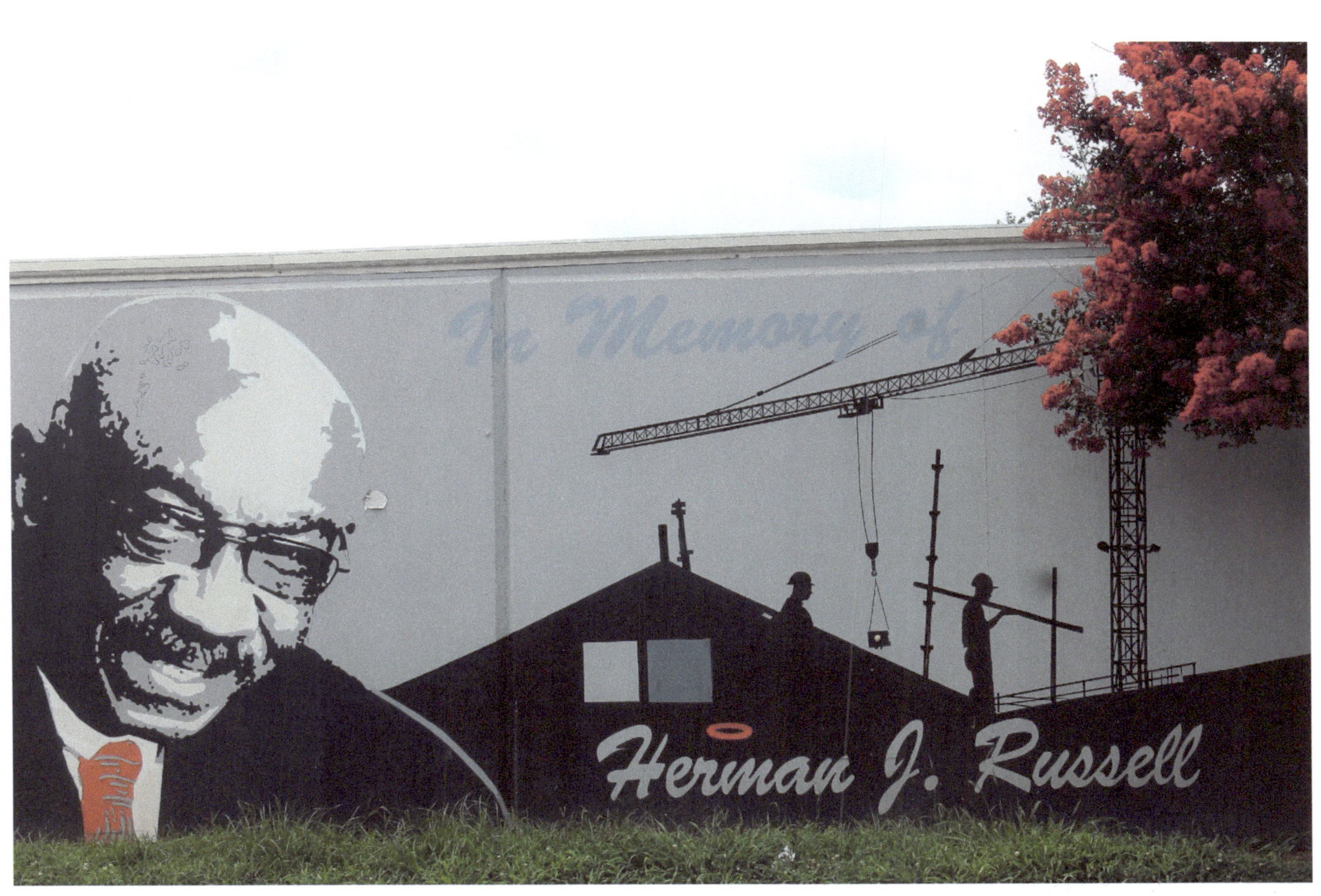
In Memory of
Herman J. Russell

Ga Peachez

Often used to make

Cobbler, Pie, Jams, and Jellies

Sweet and Juicy Treats

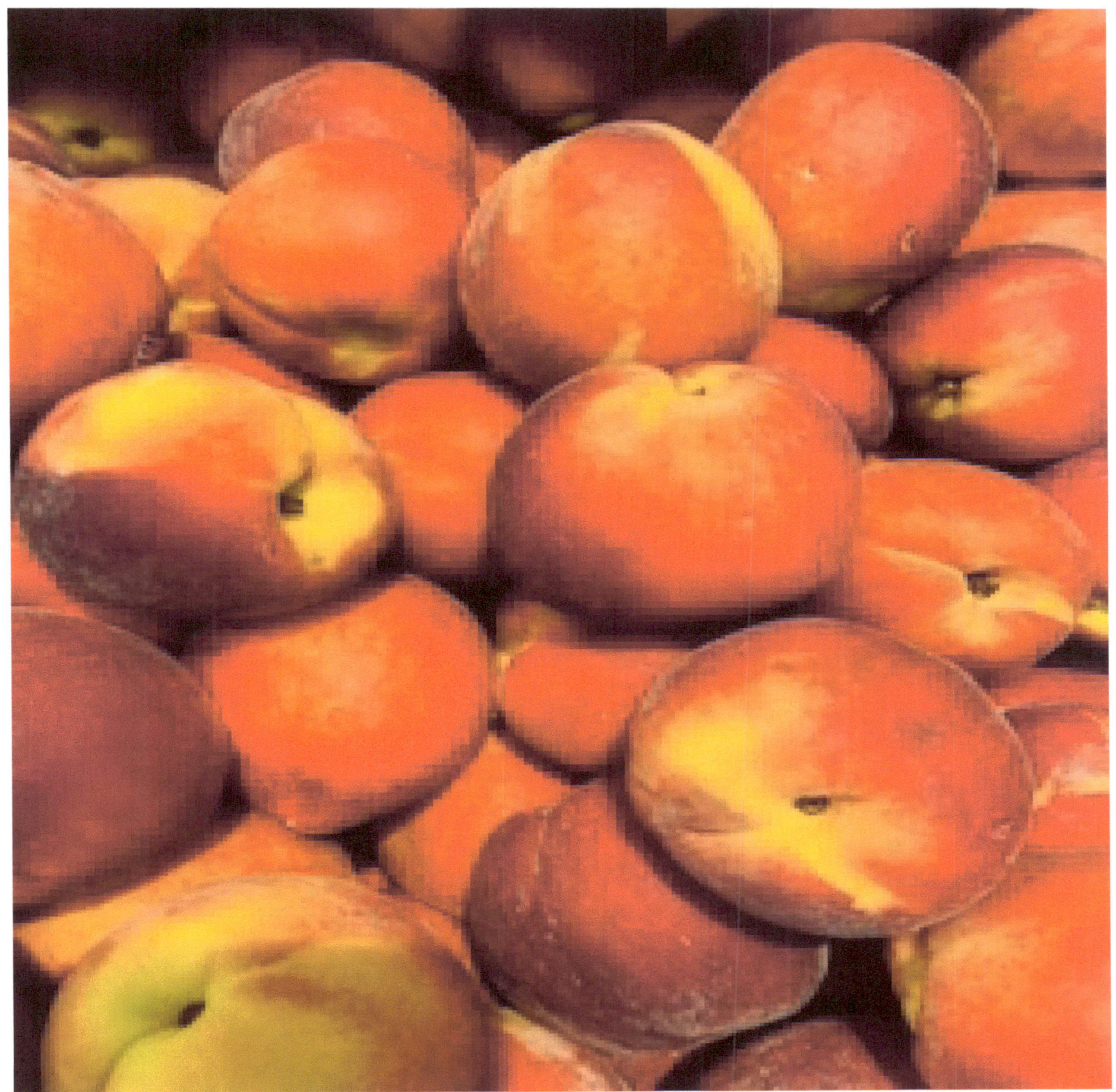

Bronze Lenz

I see Atlanta through brown eyes
Eyes that are sometimes viewed
Not as equally clear as blue

I have a different perspective than most
Different from someone raised from the West Coast
Different than someone raised south of the Macon Dixie Line

My glasses are often shaded
clouded by others hatred
I don't have the same prescription as you

I look through a bronze lenz
a lenz crafted by those who design
blurred images of my kind

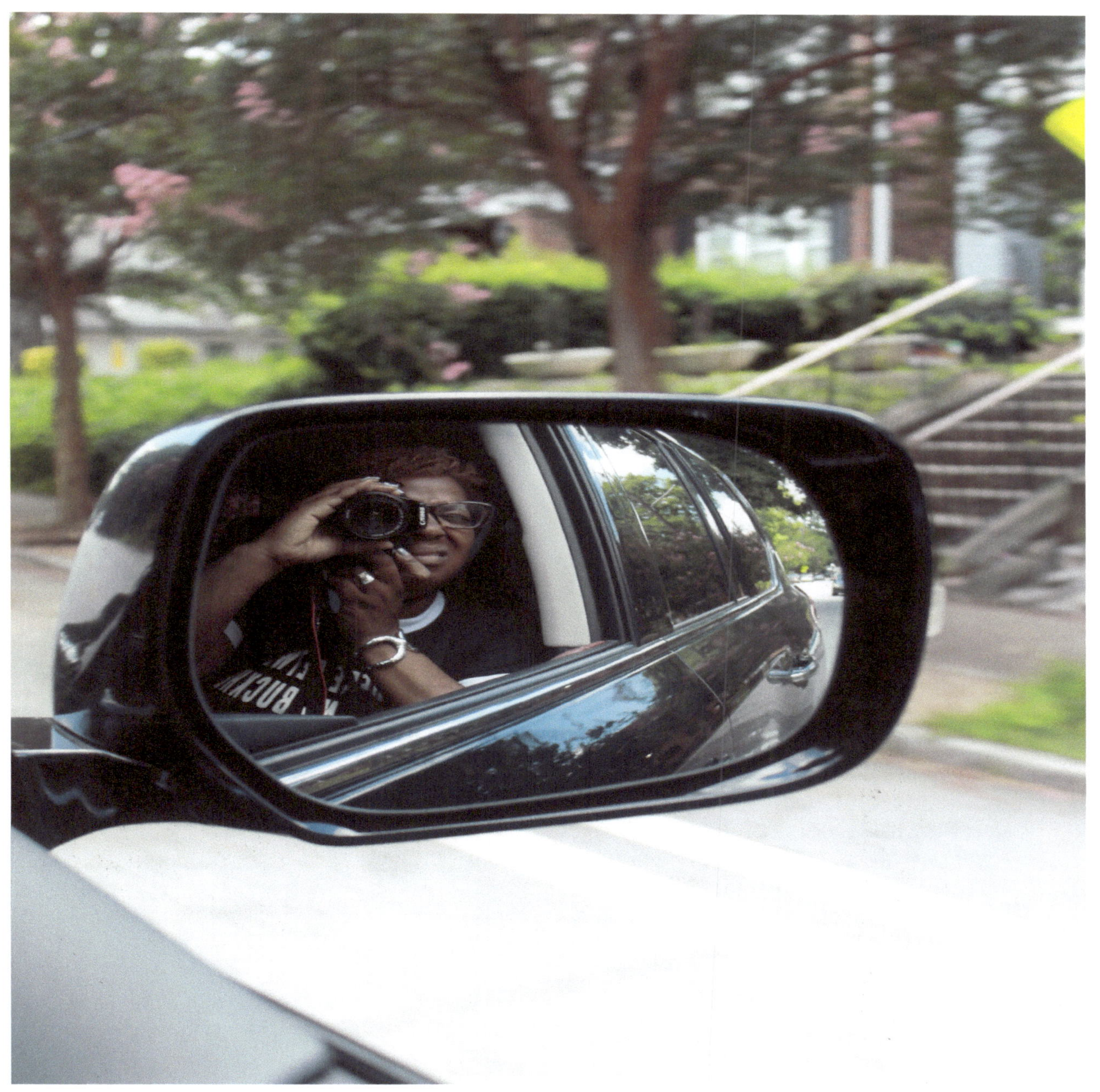

75 Dr. Martin Luther King Jr. Statue at Morehouse College
76 Chick-Fil-A College Football Hall of Fame, Atlanta
77 Willie Watkins Funeral Home
78 John Wesley Dobbs Statue, Sweet Auburn
79 Mural by Greg Mike on the Sound Table Restaurant at Edgewood and Boulevard, 2020
80 Coca Cola Clock, Atlanta
81 Birthplace of Dr. Martin Luther King Jr,, Auburn Avenue
82 Cafe Hot Wing
83 Civil Rights Mural by Artist Muhammad Yungai, Boone Blvd, Atlanta
84 Chenault Homes
85 Marta Station on Lowery Blvd, Mural by Artist Fahamu Pecou
86 Decatur Charlez, South Dekalb Mall, Decatur GA
87 The Skyview Ferris Wheel, Atlanta
88 West End Mall, Atlanta
89 Shopping Carts of the Homeless, Atlanta
90 The Gold Dome, Atlanta City Capitol Building
91 Grafitti Bridge on Boulevard
92 Hartsfield Airport North Terminal
93 ATL Decor @ Macys in Lennox Mall
96 Protest Signs photo by Tara Thieleke
97 Protestors photo by Tara Thieleke
99 Interstate 285
102 Ebenezer Baptist Church
103 Wheat Street Baptist Church
105 Hollywood Road, NW Atlanta
107 Friends at the Trap Museum, Atlanta
109 Segue Tour, Savannah GA
111 The Old Kessler's Downtown Atlanta GA
113 Author at Atlanta Brewing Company, Atlanta photo taken by Paige Hutchinson
115 Mural of Evelyn Gibson Lowery, SCLC/WOMEN Auburn Ave (Loss Prevention Artists)
117 Outkast Mural by JEKS, Little Five Points Atlanta, photo by Bedarius Bell, Jr.
119 Freaknik Concert 2019
121 The Fabulous Fox Theatre, Downtown Atlanta
123 Mural of Herman J. Russell, Haynes Street (Loss Prevention Artists)
125 Georgia Peaches@ Walmart, Lithonia
127 Self Portrait
132 Community Roots Mural by Muhammad Yungai in Castleberry Hill, Atlanta

Special Thanks…

To God for giving me a creative purpose in life

To my Mom, Catherine the Great, my biggest cheerleader, for always supporting me

To my sisters and diehard ATLiens who drove me around Atlanta to get my photos and brainstormed with me on the definitions of black@lanta and who agreed to be apart of this project I appreciate you beyond measure. Thanks for editing, critiques, and being my #1 fans.

The ATLien Crew
Deria Whatley, Charcia Nichols, Kendrallynn Edwards, Charles Marable, L.D. Wells

Models
Deria Whatley, Kendrallynn Edwards, Charles Marable, Donna High Brown, Lydia Howard Powell, Janea Johnson, Kimberly Manning, Marvette Davis, Ayanna Card, Makenzie Crossman and Sereniti Harris

Thanks to my photography team and graphic artists and videographer
Fatima Young of Fatima Michon Photography

Ayanna Card of Plain Jane Visuals and www.needthattee.com

Rashid McGriff Videographer

Other Photographers who contributed
Bedarius Bell, Jr.
Paige Hutchinson
Tara Thieleke
Calvin Thomas
L.D. Wells

About the Author

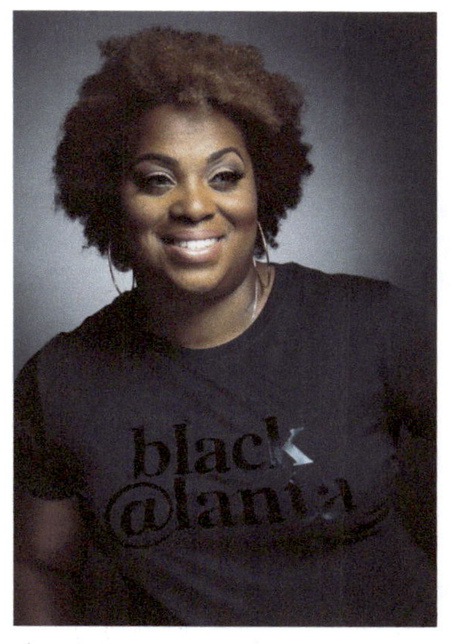

Dr. Francene Amaris Breakfield (Fran) is a native of Atlanta Georgia. Her gift of giving back makes her a beacon to all those she comes in contact with through her creative and artistic God given talents. Currently, she serves as a School Counselor at a local high school in the Metro Atlanta area and has been an educator for over twenty years. Fran has also served as an athletic and performance coach (competition cheerleading, Girl's Track and Field, and Stepping). She is a 2015 Class Noble Educator of Distinction, a 2016 National Council of Negro Women (NCNW) Trailblazer in Education Award recipient, and a 2017 Nominee for Georgia School Counselor of the Year. Fran is truly gifted working with children but her passion is painting and creative writing. She recently opened her own art instruction business and is the co-editor of the award winning book, An Anthology of Sisterhood.

Fran received her Bachelor Degree in Psychology from the University of Georgia, a Masters of Education in Counselor Education from Georgia Southern University, an Educational Specialist in School Counseling from Georgia State University, and a Doctor of Education in Curriculum Studies from Georgia Southern University. Her research centers around sisterhood and mentoring experiences of African American women.

Fran holds a certification from Emory University in the area of creative writing. She is proud of her first children's book Proud to be a PK which was released in 2019. The fourth publication of this acclaimed author is a coffee table book of poetry centered around black Atlanta. The book shares the Black Mecca through the eyes of an Atlanta native. Fran enjoys cultural experiences around cities locally, nationally and internationally. She resides in Lithonia, Georgia with her four legged fur baby, Simba.

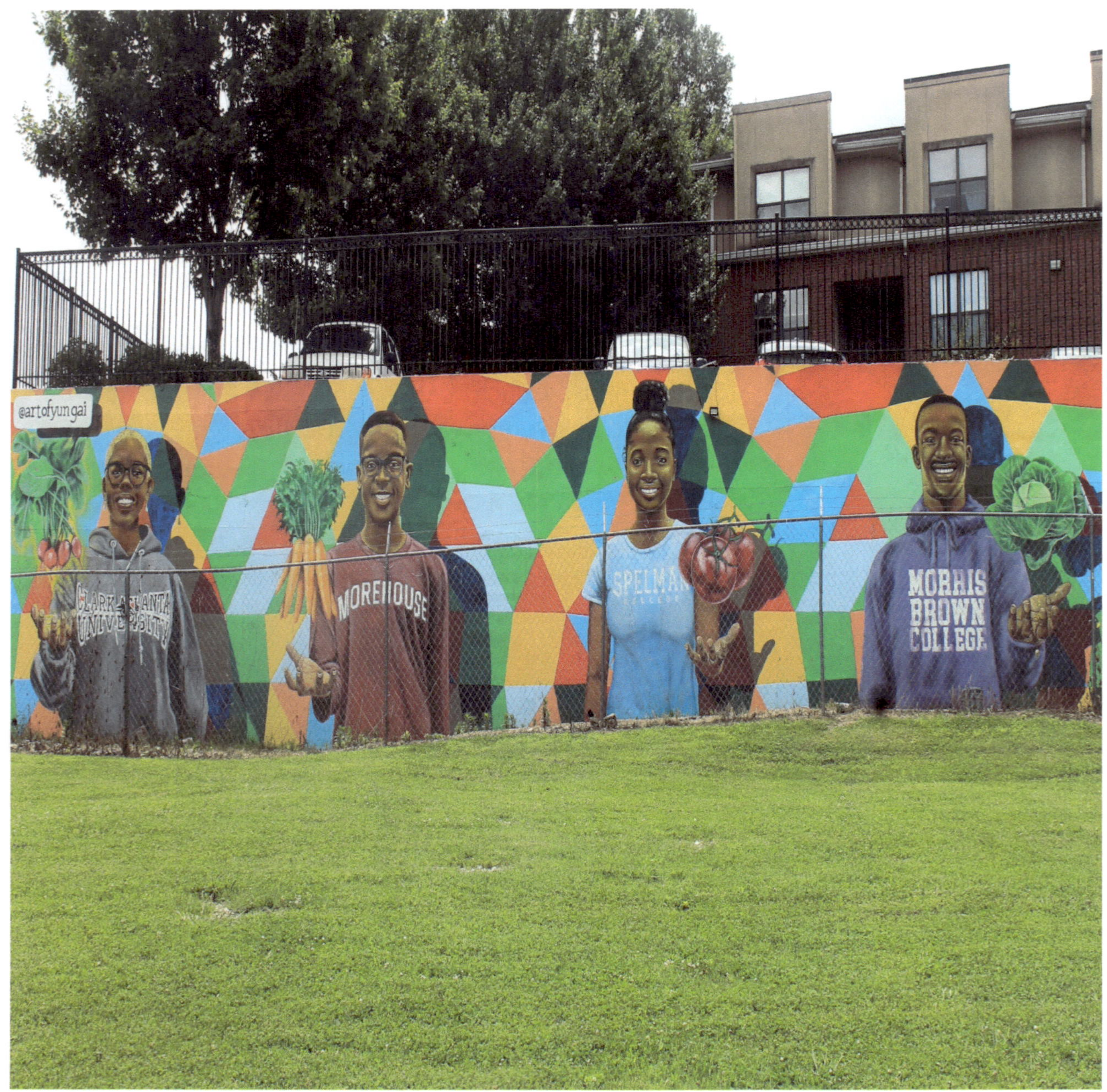
@artofyungai
MOREHOUSE
SPELMAN
MORRIS
BROWN
COLLEGE

www.ingramcontent.com/pod-product-compliance
Lightning Source LLC
LaVergne TN
LVHW070125110826
845147LV00002B/191

* 9 7 8 0 5 7 8 7 0 8 4 7 8 *